THE POPULAR

Also by Paul Preston
THE COMING OF THE SPANISH CIVIL WAR
SPAIN, THE EEC AND NATO (*with Denis Smyth*)
THE TRIUMPH OF DEMOCRACY IN SPAIN
THE SPANISH CIVIL WAR
THE SPANISH RIGHT IN THE TWENTIETH CENTURY,
AUTHORITARIANISM, FASCISM AND MILITARY CONSPIRACY

The Popular Front in Europe

Edited by

Helen Graham

Lecturer in the Department of Spanish, Portuguese and Latin American Studies
University of Southampton

Paul Preston

Professor of Modern History
Queen Mary College, University of London

MACMILLAN
PRESS

First edition 1987
Reprinted 1989

Published by
THE MACMILLAN PRESS LTD
Houndmills, Basingstoke, Hampshire RG21 2XS
and London
Companies and representatives
throughout the world

Printed in Hong Kong

British Library Cataloguing in Publication Data
The Popular Front in Europe.
1. Popular fronts—History
I. Graham, Helen   II. Preston, Paul, 1946–
320.94   HX40
ISBN 0–333–40660–5 (hardcover)
ISBN 0–333–48425–8 (paperback)

Contents

Notes on the Contributors

Helen Graham lectures in the Department of Spanish, Portuguese and Latin American Studies, University of Southampton. She is editor (with Martin Alexander) of *The French and Spanish Popular Fronts: Comparative Perspectives* and has recently completed a D.Phil on the eclipse of the Spanish Socialist Party during the civil war.

Jonathan Haslam is a Senior Research Fellow in Politics at King's College, Cambridge. He was Visiting Associate Professor of History at Stanford (1986–87) and Visiting Associate Professor of Political Science at the University of California, Berkeley (1987–88). He is the author of *Soviet Foreign Policy, 1930–33*, *The Soviet Union and the Struggle for Collective Security in Europe, 1933–39*, and *The Soviet Union and the Politics of Nuclear Weapons in Europe, 1969–87*.

Martin Kitchen is Professor of History at the Simon Fraser University, Burnaby, Canada. He is the author of *Fascism*, *The Coming of Austrian Fascism*, *British Policy towards the Soviet Union during the Second World War*, and *The Origins of the Cold War in Comparative Perspective* (with Lawrence Aronsen).

David A. L. Levy formerly taught French politics and history at the University of Salford. His D.Phil thesis, 'The Marseilles Working Class, 1936–38', was presented in 1982. He now works for the BBC.

Paul Preston is Professor of Modern History and Director of the Centre for Contemporary Spanish Studies at Queen Mary College, University of London. He is the author of *The Coming of the Spanish Civil War* and *The Triumph of Democracy in Spain*.

Stephen Salter is a Lecturer in the Department of History, University of Sheffield, with research interests in twentieth-century German history.

Donald Sassoon lectures in history at Westfield College, University of London. He is the editor of *On Gramsci and Other Writings* and the author of *The Strategy of the Italian Communist Party*, *Contemporary Italy* and numerous articles on Italian politics and history.

List of Abbreviations

ASM	the Madrid section of the Spanish Socialist Party
CEDA	the Spanish Confederation of Autonomous Rightist Groups –mass clerical–conservative party.
CGT	French Trade Union Confederation (anarcho–syndicalist to 1914, socialist 1921 to early 1936, socialist and communist 1936 onwards)
CGTU	French Communist Trade Union Federation (1921 to early 1936)
CNT	Spanish anarcho–syndicalist trade union
DDP	German Democratic Party (left liberal)
DVP	German People's Party (conservative)
FJS	Spanish Socialist Party's youth movement which amalgamated with the communist youth in April 1936
FNTT	landworkers' section of the UGT (see below)
KPD	German Communist Party
KPÖ	Austrian Communist Party
NSBO	Nazi Labour Front
NSDAP	German National Socialist Party (Nazis)
PCE	Spanish Communist Party
PCF	French Communist Party
PCI	Italian Communist Party
POUM	left communist dissident party in Spain
PSI	Italian Socialist Party
PSOE	Spanish Socialist Party
SFIO	French Socialist Party
SPD	German Social Democratic Party
SPÖ	Austrian Social Democratic Party
UGT	Spanish Trade Union Federation (socialist)

1 The Popular Front and the Struggle Against Fascism

Helen Graham and Paul Preston

One of the more bizarre consequences of the Bolshevik revolution was that the years from 1918 to 1939 were an era of virtually uninterrupted working-class defeat. There were innumerable heroic episodes but the overall trend was catastrophic. The crushing of revolution in Germany and Hungary after the First World War was followed by the destruction of the Italian Left by Mussolini, the establishment of dictatorships in Spain and Portugal and the defeat of the General Strike in Britain. The rise of Hitler saw the annihilation of the most powerful working-class movement in Western Europe, and within a year the Austrian Left suffered a similar fate. Austria stands out because there, for the first time, workers took up arms against fascism, in 1934. Tragically, it was too late and the domino effect continued across central Europe.

When the Spanish Civil War broke out in 1936, it was only the latest and fiercest battle in a European civil war which had been under way since the Bolshevik triumph of 1917. There had been signs of it even before 1914 in the increasingly bitter trade union struggles fought in Britain, France, Russia and Germany. The First World War and mass conscription altered the relation of forces in most countries. Labour shortages strengthened the hand of the unions while social dislocation, scarcity, inflation and the scale of casualties borne by the working class intensified mass militancy.[1] In one country, Russia, there was an outright victory for the Left and all over Europe the Right drew its own conclusions. Russia had become both a threat, intensifying fears of working-class revolution, and a target, accelerating the search for new methods of political defence, the most spectacular of which was to be fascism. Allied intervention against the fledgling Soviet Union and the savage repression of the left-wing movements in Germany, Hungary and Italy were all part of a reaffirmation of bourgeois Europe. There is no denying the strength of the old order or the resilience of bourgeois forces in forging new weapons against revolutionary threats.[2] However, the successive defeats of the working class cannot be explained only in terms of the power of the enemy.

The Bolshevik experience, while perhaps providing a symbol of hope for many workers, had ultimately weakened the international workers'

1

movement. The most bitter divisions followed the creation in 1919 of the Communist International, its imposition of rigid policies on individual communist parties – irrespective of national realities – and its blatant efforts to poach socialist militants by dint of smear campaigns against their leaders. All these factors severely diminished the capacity of European labour and the Left to meet the right-wing onslaught stimulated by 1917. Convinced of the inevitability of the collapse of capitalism, the Comintern's leaders saw social democrats not as possible allies against fascism but as obstacles to revolution. While the European Right reacted with hysterical fear to the mere idea of the Comintern, the communists, confident that fascism was doomed along with the capitalism that spawned it, concentrated their fire on the socialists. At its Sixth Congress in 1928, the policy of 'class against class' was adopted and with it the notion that social democrats would try to divert the working class from its revolutionary mission and were therefore 'social fascists'.

With the triumph of Stalin's notion of 'socialism in one country', world revolution had taken a back seat in Soviet calculations. Its warriors had increasingly dropped back to become the frontier guards of the 'first workers' state'. Russia's appalling economic problems, combined with Stalin's instinctive insularity, ensured that he regarded the Comintern with an indifference bordering on contempt. By 1930, the leadership of the Comintern was dealing not with hypothetical prospects of future revolution but with the immediate threats of fascist aggression at national and international levels. The most damning indictments of the Comintern have centred on its share of blame for the rise of Hitler.[3] According to this argument, Hitler could have been stopped had it not been for the antagonism between the German Socialist Party (SPD) and the Communist Party (KPD). Since the run of working-class reverses was not halted, the fault lay with the Comintern because of its abusive treatment of social democracy. In fact, it appears increasingly that, in the darkest hours for the international working class, bewilderment rather than villainy was the order of the day at Comintern headquarters. As E. H. Carr has shown, it was not entirely a question of the Comintern handing down policy decisions through an iron hierarchy of local party functionaries but rather of a confused organisation under enormous pressure and riven by complex disputes and discussions.[4] Moreover, while it was true that the KPD was slavishly dependent on Moscow, socialist–communist hostility was based on more than Comintern-scripted insults. The respectable, well-housed, skilled workers of the SPD were the subject of spontaneous abuse and resentment from the young, unskilled, unemployed labourers recruited by the KPD. In addition, KPD electoral success was greatest when its 'social fascist' line was at its most apparently absurd and irrelevant.[5]

The period beginning in late 1929 with the collapse of the New York stock exchange was hailed in communist circles as heralding the final agony of capitalism, yet Moscow's reaction was far from one of unalloyed rejoicing. Apart from the immediate problems of famine conditions following in the wake of forced collectivisation, the USSR still needed economic and technological links with the advanced capitalist countries to further its own development. The crash of 1929 not only threatened those links but it also opened the door to an hysterical capitalist lashing-out against the Soviet Union. Accordingly, the search for allies among the capitalist countries became an urgent necessity. At the same time as this external context constrained the revolutionary role of the Comintern, that organisation was already bitterly divided by arguments as to its best strategy. Hard-liners like Bela Kun claimed that the communists should smash the social democratic heresy, make revolution, and thereby incapacitate the enemies of the motherland of socialism. Realists like Manuilsky argued that, in the face of fascist aggression, communists should seek collaboration with other left-wing elements. Inevitably, the debates centred on Germany.

The Comintern was puzzled by Hitler's anti-capitalist rhetoric and deceived by his hostility to the same Western powers who were the USSR's main enemies. Comintern thinking on Germany was also severely restricted by the indentification of social democracy with 'social fascism'. The KPD itself was especially sectarian and triumphalist in its conviction that 'objectively' the SPD was a more formidable defender of capitalism than the doomed Nazis. A number of factors eventually imposed a more flexible view. Growing evidence of Hitler's long-term anti-Soviet ambitions coincided with the Japanese invasion of Manchuria to persuade Moscow that France would be a better ally than Germany. The appalling truth of what Hitler's victory meant for the workers' movement boosted rank-and-file pressure in many countries for a more flexible united front policy. The advocacy of French and Spanish communists was reinforced by the prestige of Togliatti and, more crucially, Dimitrov. After his heroic performance in the *Reichstag* fire trial, the Bulgarian communist had become an international symbol of the anti-fascist struggle and, as such, carried unusual weight with Stalin. Accordingly, the Comintern came around, belatedly, to endorse the existing movement towards unity on the Left in Europe and adopted the Popular Front as its own.

Fifty years after the heyday of popular frontism, it requires little effort to perceive its attractiveness for contemporaries. The Popular Front was a device to build political unity among democratic forces, linking worker and bourgeois across barriers of social class, in order to mount domestic and international resistance to the greater common enemy of fascism and the authoritarian Right. However, the simplicity of its appeal is deceptive. Beyond the relative straightforwardness of the theoretical concept lie the ambiguities and contradictions of a strategy whose practical realisation proved ultimately impossible. In those countries – Germany, Italy and Austria, – where democracy and the workers' movement had already succumbed to fascism and the extreme Right, the concept of popular unity came too late. Yet, even in France and Spain, where it was possible to build on the lessons of Italy in 1922, of Germany in 1933 and Austria in 1934, and where bourgeois democrats and working-class parties shared power in the name of the Popular Front, it was only an interlude. The inexorable march of domestic and international fascism was held back but briefly. Moreover, between 1939 and 1941, the communist movement abandoned popular frontism as unceremoniously as it had adopted it, only to pick it up again after the German invasion of Russia.

In 1935, however, in the light of a dawning realisation of what Italian fascism and German Nazism meant for workers and democrats of all classes, large numbers of people were moved, in abstract terms at least, by the concept of political unity against a voracious fascism abroad and reactionary forces at home.[6] Unfortunately, the economic crisis of 1930s Europe, which was at the heart of the necessity for liberal and left-wing unity, was ultimately to prevent its conversion into an enduring political formula. The deteriorating economic situation in the depression years not only provided the motive power behind fascism, both for its backers – industrialists, bankers and landowners – and for its rank-and-file – the proletarianised lower middle classes and the lumpen proletariat – but it also provoked bitter and destructive tactical divisions among the forces of the Left both in and out of power. The reasons why popular frontism as an experiment in social and economic reform by parliamentary means was so easily eroded remains of considerable relevance today. That the lesson of the Popular Front in France and Spain had not been learned was tragically illustrated in the 1970s in Chile. Electoral success is not synonymous with the power necessary to introduce structural reform, or even to safeguard the democratic regime from its violent enemies. The key to the failure of the Popular Front lay in the failure of its adherents to perceive this and therefore to utilise the resources of the state to the full in defence of their own interests.

Popular unity was more easily achieved as a slogan than put into concrete practice, as the essays in this collection vividly demonstrate. In Chapter 2, on the German Left in the 1930s, Stephen Salter charts the shattering defeat of Western Europe's most powerful working-class movement at the hands of the Nazi regime. That regime would soon become, through its louring international presence, the central factor in impelling the Communist International, as the instrument of Soviet policy, to develop a strategy which would both match and foment its desire for alliance with the bourgeois powers. It has been usual to analyse the reasons for the notorious division of the German Left in the light of an international context of depression and the impact of the Comintern's divisive policies on the KPD. Dr Salter, however, poses the pertinent question of whether the German Left, divided or united, passive or on the offensive, could have countered the leviathan of Nazism in a period of acute economic crisis. It was the depression itself which disarmed the German labour movement, emasculating its only weapon in the face of the threat of mass unemployment, the militancy and solidarity of part of its base.

The notion that the rise of Nazism can be attributed exclusively to working-class divisions ignores the extent to which the German Left was isolated in the national context. There simply did not exist in the Weimar Republic in the early 1930s any remotely sufficient basis for consensus on which to build a broad, defensive cross-class alliance of the Popular Front type against both Nazism and the powerful traditional authoritarian Right. Both a pervasive anti-communism and the depth of the economic crisis drastically reduced the room for compromise between bourgeois and proletarian, and even between worker and worker. The political polarisation which ultimately led to an imposed unity on the Right in Italy, Germany and Spain, produced atomisation on the Left.

As a party steeped in constitutionalism, the German Socialist Party had the worst of all worlds. The party was an object of suspicion as far as the German Communist Party was concerned precisely because of its connections with the government. However, the rightward trend of the government by the early 1930s had equally alienated the SPD rank-and-file. The Socialist Party was rapidly becoming a political outsider. Unable to act as watchdog for the workers, the SPD could do nothing to prevent the acceleration of savage deflationary policies and cuts in social services. Therein lay the gravity of the situation. The socialists' ingrained sense of legality, order and hierarchy, together with their aged leadership structure, pilloried years before by Robert Michels as 'ossification, bossification and bourgeoisification', severely limited their power of response.[7] The socialists' party and union structures were models of the state system which they had hoped one day to inherit by peaceful means. SPD legalism precluded – indeed made inconceivable – violent, illegal resistance to the erosion of social and economic legislation. To make matters worse, as the legal structure of reform was dismantled, the very *raison d'être* of social democracy became tenuous in the extreme.

Unity on the Left in Europe between social democratic and communist parties foundered for many reasons. Most obviously, the sheer irreconcilability of their respective revolutionary and reformist stances remained a central obstacle. More crucially, given that most communist parties were born of schisms within a longer-standing socialist party, relations were soured between them. On the socialist side, there was resentment of the upstarts who had split the party. This was compounded by outrage at the subsequent efforts of the communists to poach socialist militants by the device of denouncing their leaders as bourgeois traitors to the workers' cause. The communists, on the other hand, smouldered with a sense of being outsiders, either because – as in Germany – they represented young, unskilled and often unemployed workers, or – as in Austria or in Spain before 1936 – they represented very few workers at all. In consequence, they viewed with a mixture of suspicion, disdain and superiority the social democrat 'insiders', with their influence in government circles, their investments, their pension schemes and their workers' clubs and libraries. To communists in the 1920s, social democrat efforts to mitigate proletarian misery by piecemeal social reform were objectively as bad as fascism since they diverted workers from their historic revolutionary destiny.

The crudest and cruellest image of this so-called 'Third Period' tactic presented the socialist leaders as duping the working class with a shoddy and meretricious legal reformism. In the cases of Germany and Austria, this was particularly ironic since, before annihilation at the hands of the extreme Right, the socialists' constitutional commitment was the most genuine and principled of any group in the entire political spectrum. Left alone in the democratic arena, the events of February 1934 in Vienna were the last desperate defence of the Austrian Socialist Party's constitutional gains. The reformist left was the political sector where constitutionalism ran deepest. Given the political principles, the values and even the organisational structure of social democracy in Europe, the revolutionary option of seizing power and imposing a dictatorship of the proletariat was inconceivable. Unfortunately, the middle way of empty rhetorical radicalism was adopted, with disastrous consequences – in

Italy by the 'maximalist' wing of the PSI under Serrati and in Spain by the 'Bolshevising' wing of the PSOE under Largo Caballero. Given the balance of armed force in the modern state, it is necessarily the Left which is constitutionalist. Even in the most severe economic crisis, there is no other choice. The most extreme cases of verbal revolutionism, those of Spain and Austria, constituted – and it is not at all a paradox – a last, desperate attempt to counter the erosion of the constitutional order.

In the case of Germany, the likely consequences of insurrection, given the power of the state together with the fundamental ethos of social democracy itself, render it difficult to sustain that the German leadership was wrong to have been so passive. The SPD adopted an inevitably pragmatic stance, aware both of its own limitations and of those of the political and economic situation. In October 1934, the slogan 'Better Vienna than Berlin' was the watchword of many Spanish socialists when they rose up in defence of the social and economic achievements of the Second Republic. United, as, in the end, the Austrian Left had been, the miners of Northern Spain were also defeated. Only if resistance is held to be an absolute principle can it be argued that the enormous human cost of defeat in 1934 and again in 1939 was worthwhile. This is not to say that working-class leadership should be supine but that it should have, as Indalecio Prieto of the PSOE had, a realistic sense of the balance of forces, a perception of the possible.

As in Spain, so too in Austria, as Martin Kitchen clearly demonstrates in Chapter 3: the Socialist Party for all its radical rhetoric was inveterately reformist in practice. Indeed, in both cases, the combination of radical language and reformist practice had an identical objective – the satisfaction of a wide variety of political opinions with the aim of preserving an overwhelmingly sacred party unity. Like the SPD, the Austrian Socialist Party (SPÖ) was steeped in notions of its constitutional duty and of the need to defend the Republic against right-wing violence. Indeed, other forces operating within the established parliamentary order would effectively destroy the constitution, leaving the SPÖ as its sole defender. As was the case in Germany, socialists and communists were divided not only by Comintern policy but also by communist resentment of the SPÖ's tradition of government involvement, and most especially of the party's readiness by 1932 to treat with Dollfuss as a 'lesser evil'. Like their German comrades, the Austrian socialists were making a misguided, and indeed dangerous, assumption because the bourgeois parties in both countries, shifting rightwards, were in fact willing to tolerate the attrition of political democracy, civil liberties and social legislation. For both socialist parties, a genuine Popular Front alliance that necessarily had to be forged across the class divide was rendered impossible by the rightist preferences of the liberal bourgeoisie. In Austria, the struggle for some degree of unity, including unity in defeat, would always be uniquely the concern of the parties of the Left.

With the example of the German *débâcle* before them, the socialist base in Austria was less prepared for conciliation. Dollfuss, condemned in the eyes of many of the socialist rank-and-file by his blatant authoritarian leanings and his meetings with Mussolini, was seen to be destroying the fabric of the democratic state in Austria. Nevertheless, the passivity or even bankruptcy of the leadership, criticised though it was by the moderates in the party, was perhaps nearer to an acceptance of the reality of the situation. The same was true of Otto Bauer's Engels-style plea that the armed resistance of the working class, however just the cause, was almost impossible against the modern state. The ultimate uprising in defence of the constitution on 12 February 1934 was provoked by continued government aggression. In its course, Austrian socialists and communists achieved, in the heat of battle, the unity which had hitherto eluded them. The insurrection was not the product of party policy but rather the spontaneous reaction of the rank-and-file in the face of the cumulative and drastic erosion of workers' rights and civil liberties.

The Viennese events proved yet again that the modern state's monopoly of violence effectively guaranteed it against conquest at the hands of left-wing forces. Nevertheless, the February crisis showed that the physical defeat of the organised working class, however resounding it might appear, was never total. The same point was to be made less than eight months later in Spain in the coalfields of Asturias. The miners' towns had been bombed by the Spanish airforce, their coastal towns shelled by the navy and their valleys finally overrun by the Spanish army. Yet, after their two weeks of heroic resistance, the miners' surrender was perceived, in the words of their leader, as merely 'a halt on the road'.[8] They had shown that the peaceful establishment of an authoritarian corporative state would not be permitted by the working class and their epic struggle became a potent symbol of proletarian unity and sacrifice.[9] Similarly, as the experiences of Italy and Germany, and much later those of Francoist Spain and Pinochet's Chile, were to demonstrate, no totalitarian regime of the Right ever proved capable of genuinely integrating its working class *en masse*. In Germany, passive resistance by the labour force hampered the drive towards rearmament and war preparation. In Italy and in Spain, the tactic of entryism into the official fascist and Falangist syndicates was pursued in the knowledge that the structures which were meant to integrate and control the workers could be exploited by them.

The experiences of the Italian, German and Spanish working classes after the establishment of the local variant of fascism in their countries were not dissimilar in terms of both repression and resistance. However, the scale of struggle, and thus the human cost, which preceded defeat at the hands of fascism or rightist authoritarianism casts a revealing light on the validity of popular frontism. In Spain as in Austria, an 'objective victory' was still an immediate defeat which left the socialist movement badly scarred, with its leaders either in prison or in exile, its press silenced, its unions emasculated and its rank-and-file cowed. The 'honour' of the working class was bought at a high price. The symbol of Asturias helped bring back together the bourgeois and socialist forces into what was later called the Popular Front. Yet had that unity not been broken in the first place, the circumstances which had provoked the Asturian rising might never have come about. Similarly, if that unity had been used wisely after February 1936, if the left wing of the socialist party had not played sectarian politics and thus left the government of Spain in the hands of incompetent republicans, then more working-class heroism and ultimate defeat would not have been necessary.[10] The human costs of the Spanish Civil War were to dwarf those of the Austrian and Asturian uprisings. Half a million people would die on the battlefields, hundreds of thousands suffer imprisonment, torture and execution and the socialist movement would not raise its head again for nearly forty years.[11]

It is obvious that, when the Left united itself, managed to establish links with the liberal democratic bourgeoisie and achieve governmental power, the consequences for the mass of the population and especially for the workers were immeasurably better than those which followed upon division. Accordingly, it is easy to focus on the blind egoism of the politicians and labour leaders whose factionalism bred disunity as being somehow to blame for the success of fascism. That is perhaps to forget the enormous practical and ideological obstacles to left-wing unity and the even greater difficulties in achieving inter-class alliances. Even when they were briefly possible, in France, Spain and most bizarrely in Chile – where the Popular Front reached power in 1938 with peripheral Nazi support[12] – they were rarely sustainable despite the plethora of salutory lessons from Italy, Germany and Austria. The scale of the economic crisis rendered competing class ambitions totally irreconcilable.

No better grasp of these essential contradictions has been achieved than that presented by Otto Bauer in his celebrated analysis of the relationship between reformist socialism and the rise of fascism.[13] In certain conditions, he argued, the capitalist order loses confidence, as it did in Italy after 1917, in Germany and Austria after 1918 and in Spain after 1930. If during this period capitalism is not overthrown by revolution, nor re-establishes its own domination, there follows what Bauer called a transitional condition of class equilibrium. The political form that it takes tends to be democratic, a popular republic of the German, Austrian or Spanish type which none the less rests on capitalist property relations. Such a republic leaves the landed and industrial oligarchies in control of the economy but allows the working classes a share in state power and the possibility of pursuing their own interests. The consequent gains won by the strengthened trade unions and the enactment of social legislation put burdens on capitalist production which, at a time of economic crisis, it is not prepared to bear. Accordingly, the haute bourgeoisie turns to fascism. Thus, according to Bauer, the rise of fascism came, not at the moment when capitalism was threatened by proletarian revolution, but during the period of truce or class equilibrium, after the first revolutionary flood had been checked. The turn to fascism is provoked less by capitalist fear of revolution than by a determination to depress wages, to destroy the social reforms achieved by the working class and to smash the positions of political power held by its representatives; not to suppress a revolutionary situation but to wipe out the gains of reformist socialism.

This theory was developed after the defeat of February 1934. Before that time, Bauer had been criticised by Karl Renner for radical posturing which frightened the bourgeoisie while masking the fact that he was not really a revolutionary at all. With sweeping criticism equally applicable to the Spanish socialist Left, Trotsky too had foreseen that Bauer's combination of rhetorical revolutionism and reformist practice would merely weaken the working class for the final clash with Dollfuss.[14] Trotsky's strictures were delivered in the belief that the only way to resolve the contradiction was by unequivocally revolutionary means, recreating the Bolshevik experience in each country. A potentially equally valid answer would have been the Popular Front pursued to its logical extreme. That would have meant the maintenance of unity at all costs in order to keep the apparatus of the state legally in the hands of the democratic Left and, thereafter, the determined use of the instruments of state power both to defend the workers from the consequences of the crisis and to introduce far-reaching social and economic reforms.

Significantly, the Asturian miners, having tried a revolutionary tactic, were to be the most fervent supporters of the Popular Front idea in Spain.[15]

It was certainly not a problem-free solution in any country. In France, the failure of the Popular Front did not necessarily prove the Trotskyist analysis that only full-scale revolution could resolve the crisis. Indeed, given the relation of forces in the country and the policies of the French communists, a revolutionary outcome was most unlikely.[16] The French failure proved rather that the full potential of the Popular Front idea had not been exploited. Léon Blum quickly discovered that his first, and only genuine, Popular Front administration was 'a transitional regime of class equilibrium' in which the political representatives of the working class and the liberal bourgeoisie had a mandate but found that the balance of economic power remained unchanged. Given that the economic power of the haute bourgeoisie was a crucial determinant of the effective exercise of political authority, the situation had perforce to be temporary or transitional. One or other side of the equation had to cede. That it was the Popular Front which ultimately did so was both an indication of the power of the Right and of the inadequacies of the way in which the strategy was put into practice.

The reality of economic depression which in a sense had made the Front possible, certainly reduced dramatically the new government's room for manoeuvre and innovation. The agreement at Matignon between organised labour and the French employers was the product of a particular psychological moment. The economic gains it symbolised had not been won definitively but rather conceded temporarily by industrialists intimidated by the experience of mass worker mobilisation. The employers, having recovered their nerve, were determined to recover the ground lost to the unions. Blum, seeing himself as the grand arbiter/conciliator, tried to steer a moderate middle course between radical social and economic transformation and no reform at all. Inevitably, he satisfied no one and there is a certain parallel here with the Spanish experience after February 1936. In effect, Blum's own convictions about the limitations of the 'exercise of power' led him to attempt to stabilise and make permanent a transitional process.

As David Levy shows in Chapter 4, the 'limitation' thus became a self-fulfilling prophecy because Léon Blum refused to accept the real significance of the strike wave of May and June 1936. The strikes constituted an unprecedented display of massive worker mobilisation. Blum was unable to perceive their potential as a motor of more profound and lasting social and economic change than could otherwise be achieved within the framework of a bourgeois democratic state. The prime minister's compromise, in that it left the economic strength of the French oligarchy intact, laid him open to the left socialists' accusation that his function was purely to 'manage the crisis' for French capitalism. Blum refused to challenge the entrenched economic powers in French society because he was not prepared for the social consequences. By his caution, he was objectively paving the way both for his own personal political defeat and for that of the Popular Front itself, inflicted in June 1937 by the radical senators. The 'long march' thus came to a halt almost before it was fully under way. The name Popular Front continued to be applied to subsequent governments but the reforming mission was no more.

In France, Blum and the French Socialist Party (SFIO) ceded at the point of conflict and consciously so. In Spain, the situation was more acute with intransigent landowners already resorting to violence to defend their estates from the application of social legislation. Having partially learned the lessons of Asturias, as discussed in Chapter 5, the Spanish Popular Front was more determined to prevent the blocking of reform. Accordingly, the Spanish Right quickly came to the conclusion that in order to defend its material interests it would have to fight a civil war and so resolve Bauer's equation by force. It was fear of civil war, in retrospect perhaps exaggerated, that had inhibited Blum in France. Similarly, fear of political and social polarisation would prevent him from sending either immediate material aid in the summer of 1936 or regular assistance thereafter to the beleaguered sister Popular Front government in Spain.[17]

In Italy, although the road to unity was to be a long and difficult one, the news of the French socialist–communist pact of July 1934 had a tremendous impact on the grass roots of the Italian Communist Party. Already many PCI members, as emigrant labourers, had experienced at first hand the enormous groundswell of pro-unity sentiment in France. As Donald Sassoon points out in Chapter 7, Togliatti himself was extremely impressed by the PCF's adoption of the Popular Front. As a senior Comintern figure, however, he remained circumspect about publicly supporting Thorez until Moscow had unequivocally endorsed the new strategy. In Spain, the idea of an inter-class alliance, albeit without the involvement of the Communist Party, pre-dated developments in France. Given the dominance of the Right in Spain, liberal republicans and socialists had been thrown into alliance as far back as 1909. The hard determination with which the Right opposed reform after 1931, however, caused important sections of the socialist movement to lose faith in the efficacy of bourgeois democracy. When the Right won the elections of 1933 against a divided Left, the aggression that it displayed in dismantling the reforms of the Second Republic led first to the desperate revolutionism of 1934 and then to a more sober reappraisal of alliance tactics in 1935.

Accordingly, pressure from the base in various countries, but most particularly in France, began to have an impact on the development of Comintern policy. As Jonathan Haslam reiterates, the evolution towards the adoption of popular frontism for individual national communist parties was closely linked to what was seen as the policy's international validity. The notion of Popular Front as espoused by the Comintern at the Seventh Congress in 1935 was a *volte-face* in its policy. With little explanation and less recantation, the divisive 'social fascism' line was replaced by a strategy of class collaboration. The reasons for this about-turn cannot be separated from domestic political developments in the Soviet Union. The Popular Front was a useful weapon with which Stalin could berate the revolutionary proletarian internationalism of his opponents. It was also a response to local pressure from French, German and even British communists. None the less, the brusque way in which the Popular Front was adopted without reference to the abandonment of the previous 'class against class' policy was symptomatic of the essential weakness of the Comintern. Particularly in countries like the United States where the communists were few, the crude imposition of popular frontism merely emphasised their dependence on Moscow. Far from heralding a new era of working-class unity, it was only a 'short aborted interlude'.[18] The general staff of world revolution were even more starkly exposed as the frontier guards of the Soviet Union when the Popular Front was dropped during the Ribbentrop–Molotov Pact.

Togliatti saw the problems involved in such violent zig-zags, as no doubt did others. Unsurprisingly, given the political climate, no Comintern leader was prepared in 1935 to push for a public debate of the inadequacies of the 'class against class' and 'social fascist' orientations. As Jonathan Haslam suggests, hopes that popular frontism would provide a degree of autonomy for the Comintern could never have been realised. The overriding needs of Soviet defence ensured that the Comintern would be tightly controlled as an instrument to bring about the isolation of Nazi Germany. The Popular Front idea was to be exploited to accustom bourgeois politicians to the notion of collaboration with communists. Once the national contradictions were exposed in France, and most starkly in Spain, the credibility of the policy was irrevocably damaged in the eyes both of the socialists and the erstwhile bourgeois allies.

In any case, the Popular Front's removal of the destructive conflicts between reformism and revolution did little to diminish tension between socialists and communists whether clandestine or open. This was most apparent in the countries where the Popular Front assumed governmental power. In both France and Spain, the most bitter rivalry was organisational. The socialists had hoped to welcome back to the fold the dissidents who had broken away between 1919 and 1921. The communists, however, hoped to take over the rank-and-file of the socialist parties and transform themselves from small cadre parties to mass parties. The Spanish socialists told their communist counterparts that 'the Communist International is interested in fostering closer relations with the socialist parties not because they may be leftist or rightist but because they control the masses'.[19] Far from relinquishing their radical heritage, the communist parties sought to exploit the mythology of Bolshevism in order to attract the left wings of the socialist movements.[20]

A further and more dangerous contradiction of the Popular Front lay in the incompatibility of the economic aspirations of its component class elements. The political aspirations of what might be termed the social base of the Popular Front – the proletariat which had given it electoral victory – had to be reckoned with. As is made clear in Chapters 4 and 6, those rank-and-file aspirations were for more radical social and economic change than the leftists in government either intended or considered realistic in the circumstances. Moreover, they went far beyond the threshold of change considered as acceptable by the liberal bourgeoisie and its political representatives.

In France, the image of the entire nation as 'Third Estate', bound in common cause by exploitation by a narrow oligarchy, fell down before the fierce conflicts of economic interest within the Front itself. As David Levy indicates, the Radicals were extremely uncertain as to what the social and economic content of the Popular Front should be. In many cases, they were 'terrified of the adventure'. In Spain, economic and political polarisation was more acute. It was not even a case of persuading the bourgeoisie to cooperate in mitigating the more inhumane aspects of capitalism in crisis, but rather one of carrying out a massive effort of structural modernisation against the wishes of a violent and reactionary oligarchy. The bourgeoisie was weak and numerically insignificant, inadequate either as a buffer between oligarchy and proletariat or as an ally of the working class. Like the radicals in France, the Spanish republicans believed that the fact of electoral victory itself rendered the mass movement superfluous. Indeed, for them, popular mobilisation signified the unacceptably dangerous face of the Front, a mere step from revolution. When popular aspirations overflowed the barriers of the Front, the land occupations in southern Spain and the strike waves of the summer of 1936 in France and Spain, employers and the liberal bourgeois politicians questioned the ability of the Front to contain and control its own electoral base.

In contrast, both the French and Spanish Communist Parties were anxious to maintain the mass mobilisations of the electoral campaigns even after victory had been achieved. In both cases the motive was the same: to sustain a situation which augmented their political influence. Nevertheless, both parties were confronted by proletarian masses whose radicalism was getting out of control. In the fields, the streets and the factories, they were demanding a level of social and economic transformation far in excess of what was considered politically expedient. Given the wider needs of Soviet policy, it was crucial that the communists did not let revolutionism get out of hand to a point where it would alarm the French bourgeoisie or the British who had investments in Spain. Accordingly, communist moderation came to exceed that of the socialists. In Spain, the exigencies of war protected the party from rank-and-file revulsion but in France some militants did choose to leave the party in protest.

The Spanish Communist Party (PCE) adopted an extremely conservative position in the face of the social and economic revolution which greeted the military coup of 17–18 July 1936. Moreover, as the symbol of Russian aid to Spain, the party was swamped with new members, becoming a middle-class, professional affair. The ubiquitousness and ruthlessness of the PCE eventually led to the alienation of the very groups – the moderate socialists and the much debilitated republican parties – to whose Popular Front the communists had anxiously attached themselves in late 1935. The revolutionary Left, appalled both by the destruction of the social and economic advances of the early months of the war and by the Stalinist witch-hunt against Left dissidents, had long since become the bitter enemy of the communists.

By the end of the civil war, the Spanish Communist Party was isolated, unable to mobilise any class behind the Popular Front it continued to uphold. This produced a variety of more or less self-critical comments from the leadership which echoed Togliatti's earlier advice that there was a need to establish much better links with the masses and to involve them in the fight against fascism to a much greater degree than had been attempted in either France or Spain. That such a strategy could

have been put forward in the later stages of the Spanish Civil War, after
the crushing of mass working-class aspirations, is an indication of the
reality of the Popular Front as far as the communists were concerned. It
was, in the last analysis, a policy dictated from the centre – from the
Comintern in Moscow – and imposed irrespective of its applicability to
individual national political realities. In some cases, at certain moments,
it was a policy which made sense in spite of manifold difficulties. In
others, the dogged refusal to modify the content of the policy because of
the needs of Moscow wrought havoc. Such was the case in Spain, where
ironically the communists had played only the most marginal role in
creating the Popular Front.

Between July and December 1936 there existed in Spain mass popular
involvement in the struggle against fascism. Unfortunately for those
who espoused the Popular Front strategy and, above all, for Soviet
foreign-policy makers, it was a mass revolutionary involvement.
Therefore, it had to be destroyed in order to promote the kind of
conventional war effort which might foster an atmosphere conducive to
the achievement of collective security. The popular revolution was,
therefore, for good or ill, destroyed and with it mass participation in a
war both against Spanish reaction and against international fascism.
Revolutionary initiatives were deemed to be objectively harmful to the
long-term interests of the world revolution as defined by Moscow.
Accordingly, the Spanish revolution had to be liquidated. Given the
notorious military weaknesses of the revolutionary militias and an
international context in which the Western allies were thought to be
anxious for any excuse to turn against the Soviet Union, this policy was
neither absurd nor illogical. However, in consequence, it was soon to
prove impossible to remobilise the proletariat in defence of a reconstituted bourgeois state in the name of the Popular Front. The
Comintern's representatives and the leadership of the PCE were to be
heard bewailing the scale of popular alienation.

It was in Spain also that the attempt to implement what might be seen
as the ultimate conclusion of the Popular Front in the form of 'national
reconciliation', further alienated other leftist political forces. The PCE
was accused of proposing the effective negation of the *raison de guerre,*
the conflict for which so many had already sacrificed their lives. In
somewhat different circumstances, reconciliation, later to be national
unity, was the policy also being pursued by the Italian Communist Party
from the mid-1930s onwards.[21] The watchword was Togliatti's exhorta-
tion to unite 'all the oppositions to fascism. This is now for us the
problem of the Popular Front.'

In Italy, this strategy was viewed with some equanimity in that it was perceived as a way of achieving dialogue with dissidents within the fascist movement. In Spain, however, in the later stages of the civil war, the PCE's calls for the 'unity of the Spanish people' across the battle lines fell on extremely deaf or extremely angry ears. The rationalisation behind it – that it would thereby isolate what was presented as the narrow fascistic clique that was allegedly Franco's only support – was self-evidently absurd. It is certainly the case that many people who found themselves in the nationalist zone during the civil war were frightened or coerced into 'geographical loyalty'. Nevertheless, the evidence of right-wing electoral performances up to 1936, and the numbers of people who flocked to the nationalist flag, constituted ample proof that Franco enjoyed the backing of more than a clique. The PCE was to relaunch the notion in the 1940s as Unión Nacional, in the 1950s as Reconciliación Nacional, and in the 1960s as the Pact for Liberty. Not until the early 1970s did the reality of Franco's Spain begin to correspond to the theory.[22] By then, popular frontism had been shorn of its Trojan horse elements and become Eurocommunism.

The credibility problems faced in the 1970s by French and Spanish, if not Italian, Eurocommunists had much to do with the legacy of mistrust left by the Popular Front in Spain during the civil war. In a sense, the wheel which had started to turn in 1917 came full circle in Spain. The Bolshevik revolution had both created the *raison d'être* of fascism and, through the divisions imposed in 1919, diminished the capacity of the international working class to resist it. Eventually, the reality of fascism created a groundswell of rank-and-file sentiment in favour of unity. Finally, the Comintern, impelled in large part, albeit not exclusively, by the needs of Soviet foreign policy, acquiesced in the idea of the Popular Front. To espouse alliance with both bourgeois liberals and social democrats was an extraordinary leap for a party which had hitherto attacked both from the heights of its revolutionary purity. The contradictions were too heavy for the edifice of popular frontism to bear. In neither France nor Spain did the bourgeois liberals ultimately have the stomach for the fight they had got themselves into. The communists, bound by the exigencies of Moscow, were too keen to pander to those bourgeois liberals to be able to permit the radical policies which might have maintained popular enthusiasm for the Front. Thus, what could have been the most efficacious barrier against fascism ultimately failed. Yet fifty years on, mistakes and contradictions aside, it is well to remember and to understand the idea, in whose name great collective and individual sacrifices like the sending of the International Brigades to Spain, were made.

Notes

1. Anthony L. Cardoza, *Agrarian Elites and Italian Fascism: The Province of Bologna 1901–1934* (Princeton, 1982) pp. 209–34; Paul Corner, *Fascism in Ferrara 1915–1925* (Oxford, 1975) pp. 28–47; Martin Clark, *Antonio Gramsci and the Revolution that Failed* (New Haven, 1977) pp. 13–35; Jügen Kocka, *Facing Total War: German Society 1914–1918* (Leamington Spa, 1984) pp. 40–67; Gerald D. Feldman, *Army, Industry and Labour in Germany 1914–1918* (Princeton, 1966) pp. 301–61, 375–404; Jürgen Tampke, *The Ruhr and Revolution* (London, 1979) pp. 33–66; Dick Geary, *European Labour Protest 1848–1939* (London, 1981) pp. 134–47; Arthur Marwick, *The Deluge: British Society and the First World War* (Harmondsworth, 1967) pp. 72–80, 218–25.

2. Arno J. Mayer, *The Persistence of the Old Regime* (London, 1981) *passim;* Charles S. Maier, *Recasting Bourgeois Europe* (Princeton, 1975) *passim.*

3. Ruth Fischer, *Stalin and German Communism* (London, 1948) *passim;* Franz Borkenau, *World Communism* (Ann Arbor, 1962) pp. 337–47; Arthur Koestler *The God That Failed* (London, 1950) pp. 43–63. For a modern account of German communist zig-zags, see Ben Fowkes, *Communism in Germany under the Weimar Republic* (London, 1984) pp. 145–71.

4. E. H. Carr, *The Twilight of Comintern 1930–1935* (London, 1982) pp. 3–32.

5. Eve Rosenhaft, *Beating the Fascists? The German Communists and Political Violence 1929–1933* (Cambridge, 1983) pp. x–xi and *passim;* Geary, *European Labour Protest,* pp. 168–71.

6. See the editor's introduction in Jim Fyrth (ed.), *Britain, Fascism and the Popular Front* (London, 1985) pp. 11–20. For a less euphoric view, see Ben Pimlott, *Labour and the Left in the 1930s* (Cambridge, 1977) pp. 77–106.

7. Robert Michels, *Political Parties: A Sociological Study of the Oligarchical Tendencies of Modern Democracy* (New York, 1915) *passim.*

8. Manuel Grossi Mier, *La insurrección de Asturias,* 2nd edn (Gijon, 1978) p. 127.

9. On the insurrection itself, the most detailed modern accounts are Paco Ignacio Taibo II, *Historia General de Asturias,* volumes 7 and 8, *Octubre 1934: el ascenso* and *Octubre 1934: la caída* (Gijon, 1978) and various authors, *Octubre 1934* (Madrid, 1985). On the origins, see Adrian Shubert, *Hacia la revolución: orígenes sociales del movimiento obrero en Asturias 1860–1934* (Barcelona, 1984). On the consequences, see Paul Preston, *The Coming of the Spanish Civil War* (London, 1978) Ch. 5.

10. See the chapter by Helen Graham in this volume; Preston, *The Coming of the Spanish Civil War,* pp. 190–9; Santos Juliá, *La izquierda del PSOE (1935–1936)* (Madrid, 1977) pp. 31–44, 279–86.

11. On repression and resistance during the Franco regime, see Paul Preston, 'The Anti-Francoist Opposition: The Long March to Unity', in Preston (ed.), *Spain in Crisis: Evolution and Decline of the Franco Regime* (Hassocks, 1976) pp. 125*ff.* On the eclipse of the Socialist Party, see Paul Preston, 'Decadencia y resurgimiento del PSOE durante el régimen franquista', *Anales de Historia,* vol. 1, 1986 (Madrid).

12. Brian Loveman, *Chile: The Legacy of Hispanic Capitalism* (New York, 1979) pp. 275–6.

13. Otto Bauer, 'Fascism', in Tom Bottomore and Patrick Goode (eds), *Austro Marxism* (Oxford, 1978) pp. 167–86; 'Las enseñanzas de la catastrofe austriaca', in *Boletín de la Unión General de Trabajadores*, March 1934; 'La insurrección obrera de Austria', in *Leviatán*, no. 2, June 1934.
14. Leon Trotsky, 'A Letter to an Austrian', 'Austria's Turn Next', 'What Must the Austrian Social Democratic Opposition Do?', in *Writings of Leon Trotsky 1932–1933* (New York, 1972) pp. 146–56, 226–31, 269–71. On the Spanish parallels, see Paul Preston, 'The Struggle Against Fascism in Spain: *Leviatán* and the Contradictions of the Socialist Left, 1934–1936', in *European Studies Review*, vol. 9 (1979) no. 1.
15. Letters and documents from Asturian miners and their leaders were reprinted in *Documentos socialistas* (Madrid, 1935) pp. 115–8, 143–200, and in *Democracia*, 13, 20 September, 11 October, 8 November, 6 December 1935.
16. Fernando Claudín, *The Communist Movement From Comintern To Cominform* (Harmondsworth, 1975) pp. 198–210.
17. David Wingeate Pike, *Les français et la guerre d'Espagne* (Paris, 1975) pp. 57–68, 79–93, 105*ff*; José Mariá Borras Llop, *Francia ante la guerra civil española* (Madrid 1981) pp. 253–61, 361*ff*; Richard Alan Gordon, 'France and the Spanish Civil War', unpublished PhD thesis, Columbia University 1971, pp. 46–89, 103–70, 327–70.
18. Theodor Draper, 'The Popular Front Revisited', in *New York Review of Books*, 30 May 1985, pp. 44–50.
19. Archive of the Spanish Communist Party, microfilm XIV, 181, p. 5.
20. Marta Bizcarrondo, *Luis Araquistain y la crisis socialista en la segunda República* (Madrid, 1975) p. 407.
21. Palmiro Togliatti, 'The Communist Policy of National Unity', in D. Sassoon (ed.), *On Gramsci and Other Writings* (London, 1979) pp. 29*ff*.
22. See Paul Preston, 'The PCE's Long Road to Democracy 1954–1977', in Richard Kindersley (ed.) *In Search of Eurocommunism* (London, 1981) pp. 36*ff*.

2 The Object Lesson: The Division of the German Left and the Triumph of National Socialism

Stephen Salter

It is perhaps one of history's more tragic ironies that the organised German working class, which Lenin had expected to be the spearhead of revolution in the advanced industrialised states of Europe, and which was confronted in the early 1930s by a conservative reaction whose hostility to the organised labour movement was uniquely unambiguous, was never able to present a united opposition to Nazism and was to suffer one of the greatest political defeats in the history of modern labour movements. This chapter explores three themes: first, the failure of the social democratic and communist parties in Germany to present a united opposition to Nazism before 1933; second, the process whereby these parties were eliminated as political forces to be reckoned with; and, third, the extent to which the two parties of the Left were able to maintain underground resistance to the National Socialist regime after March 1933.

THE DIVISION OF THE LEFT BEFORE 1933

In the November 1932 elections to the *Reichstag*, which preceded Hitler's appointment as Reich Chancellor in January 1933, the National Socialist Party (NSDAP) won 33.1 per cent of the popular vote. This represented a set-back on the 37.3 per cent of the vote which the NSDAP had secured in the July 1932 elections – the height of the party's electoral success in free elections. The combined votes of the Social Democratic Party (SPD) and Communist Party (KPD) in the same two elections amounted to 36.2 per cent and 37.3 per cent of the vote.[1] At no stage before January 1933 did the NSDAP succeed in making serious inroads into the electoral constituencies of the SPD and KPD. Not only did the NSDAP have little positive to offer industrial workers after its refoundation in February 1925, but also, from 1928 onwards, as the party sought to maximise its support among those social groups which increasingly came to form its electoral basis – the 'old' and, from 1930 onwards, the 'new' lower middle classes – the content and form of its propaganda must have seemed unattractive to industrial workers. The NSDAP's calls for reductions in taxation, increases in food prices, restrictions on consumer and department stores, and a reduction in wages and social services, fell – unsurprisingly – on deaf ears among industrial working-class voters.[2] Nor, before 1933, did the NSDAP's embryonic trade union organisation – the NSBO – succeed in attracting industrial workers away from their traditional left-wing or catholic unions.[3] Yet the SPD and KPD were unable to offer any effective opposition to Hitler's appointment as Chancellor and the rapid destruction both of Weimar democracy and of their own political and trades union organisations. Two questions arise from this. Why did a united left-wing opposition to authoritarianism not emerge in Germany before 1933? What difference to the course of events would such a united opposition have made had it emerged?

It has long been a commonplace that the fundamental hostility to the Weimar Republic exhibited by the KPD, and its attacks on the SPD, were major obstacles to any kind of Popular Front between the two parties with the aim of combating the NSDAP. The disaster experienced by the Chinese Communist Party in 1927, when it was destroyed following a misguided alliance with the nationalist Kuomintang which the leadership of the Comintern had considered to be a 'progressive' force, led Stalin to conclude that collaboration with non-communist political forces was dangerous; and the onset of the world economic crisis in 1929 combined with the 'left-turn' in Soviet domestic politics to strengthen this 'ultra-leftist' line. As the economic crisis deepened, the official Comintern line – faithfully followed by the KPD leadership – was that the collapse of capitalism was both inevitable and imminent and that fascism was merely the last desperate attempt of monopoly capital to prevent this. Given the inevitable collapse of capitalism, the only barrier to a successful workers' revolution (led by the communist parties) was the attempt by social democratic parties to divert workers from engaging in the coming struggle. Hence the 'social fascism' thesis, in which social democracy was portrayed as a greater enemy of the working class than the authoritarian Right.[4] Despite the NSDAP's success in the July 1932 *Reichstag* elections, in September 1932 the executive committee of the Comintern pressed for the extension of the 'ultra-leftist' course; and considered the main objective of the KPD's activity to be the undermining of the 'social fascist' SPD from below.[5]

Yet the ultra-leftist course pursued by the KPD in the years before 1933 cannot be seen as the sole reason for the fact that a KPD–SPD Popular Front against Nazism failed to materialise. The divisions within the German labour movement went very deep, and even had the Comintern not dictated a suicidal strategy to the KPD, there would have remained considerable obstacles in the way of the Popular Front. The hostility displayed towards the Weimar Republic by the KPD, and towards the SPD as the major force supporting the Republic and participant in government throughout the Republic's history, is explicable not least in terms of the legacy of the SPD's invocation of right-wing paramilitary forces to suppress the revolutionary activities of the radical Left in 1919, and the continuing use made by the SPD in government of the forces of the state to hamper the public political activity of the KPD. In these circumstances, the statement of the leader of the KPD, Ernst Thälmann, before the April 1932 Prussian *Landtag* elections, that 'the positions occupied by the SPD in the Prussian state apparatus and elsewhere are not a weapon [at the disposal] of the working class . . . they are a weapon for the bourgeoisie . . .' may not have seemed entirely unreasonable.[6] Moreover, there is little indication that the SPD leadership would have welcomed the prospect of a defensive alliance with the KPD. If the KPD saw in the SPD leadership the allies of the Right in 1919, the SPD saw the KPD as a political force implacably hostile to the republican order with which it, the SPD, was strongly identified at all political levels – regional and local as well as national. Throughout the history of the Weimar Republic, the SPD at both regional and national level remained virulently anti-communist, expelling communists from public office and, for example, banning communist-inspired demonstrations.[7]

In addition to these political and ideological divisions, there is also some evidence to suggest that the division of the Left reflected a deeper social division within the German working class. By late 1932, the KPD was the party of the unemployed, to whose ranks perhaps 90 per cent of its membership belonged.[8] This coincidence of a very high proportion of unemployed members and its exclusion from, and fundamental hostility to, the institutions of the Weimar Republic, had made the KPD an outsider party *par excellence* by the early 1930s. Both in terms of its participation in government and administration and commitment to the institutions of the Republic, and in terms of the relatively more favourable economic and social position for its membership, the SPD was an insider party. The possibilities for cooperation between the two parties were, accordingly, slim.

The obstacles in the way of a defensive alliance of the two major parties of the German Left in the early 1930s were, therefore, considerable. Yet there is also much evidence to suggest that even if the political and ideological gulf between the two parties could have been overcome and a defensive alliance established, this might not have significantly altered the fate of the Republic. Any such alliance would have been massively hampered by two factors: first, the catastrophic consequences of the Depression for the organised labour movement; and, second, the wider isolation of the Left from other republican political forces whose support would have been essential for the creation of a broader-based Popular Front appealing across class lines.

By 1932, national income was 40 per cent lower than it had been in 1929, and one third of the working population was unemployed. The industrial working class was particularly severely hit by the economic crisis. By 1933, 40 per cent of all industrial workers were unemployed – compared with 13 per cent of white-collar workers. The state unemployment insurance scheme broke down under the strain of having to cope with more than six million (registered) unemployed. The effects of economic recession also extended to those fortunate enough to have retained their jobs. At least 16 per cent of these were working short-time; and the state of the labour market, together with wage cuts imposed by the Brüning government, increased tax and insurance contributions and an increase in the cost of living, combined to reduce the real wages of employed industrial workers by perhaps 18 per cent. Workers were forced to work harder in order to retain their jobs, and found themselves competing with one another in the wake of mass dismissals. The impact of mass unemployment on the trade union movement was little short of catastrophic. Unemployment was concentrated in those sectors of the economy which had been strongly organised; and with over half of their members unemployed, and a substantial proportion working short-time, the unions suffered massive financial and organisational damage. Unable to prevent mass dismissals, cuts in real wages and the reorganisation of production techniques, the unions had by late 1932, to a very large extent, ceased to be able to represent their members' interests effectively. In these circumstances, it is not surprising that the majority of union leaders rejected out of hand the possibility of political strikes. Faced by a massive pool of potential strike-breakers, it was by no means certain that employed workers would have responded to a call for a political strike. This applied particularly to those workers in public employment in the transport systems, whose participation would have been crucial to the success of any such strike. The financial and organisational havoc wreaked on the labour movement by the Depression goes a long way towards explaining the relative passivity of the SPD and the central trade union leadership – the ADGB – in the face not only of the dismissal of the SPD regional government in Prussia in July 1932, but also in response to Hitler's appointment as Chancellor in January 1933 and the Nazi terror which was subsequently unleashed against the organisations of the Left.[9]

More generally, the Left remained isolated from other republican political forces whose support would have been essential for the creation of a broad alliance against Nazism and the authoritarian Right. Such support would have had to have come from two sources: first, the Catholic Zentrum or Centre Party; and, second, from the centrist republican parties. All the available evidence suggests that support from either of these quarters for a putative defensive alliance simply would never have materialised. The anti-communism of the Zentrum was little short of that exhibited by the authoritarian Right; and the rightward orientation of the party had become more pronounced with the appointment of Kaas, a priest, as its leader in autumn 1928, and with the parliamentary delegation of the party being led by Brüning.[10] The deflationary policies pursued by the Brüning government between March 1930 and May 1932, and the SPD's parliamentary 'toleration' of these, was a major obstacle to any cooperation between the SPD and the KPD; and the attitude of the Zentrum both before and after Hitler's appointment as Chancellor – concerned as it was first and foremost to defend the institutional position of Catholics in Germany – precluded any possibility of cooperation against the authoritarian Right. Thus, whilst the Zentrum retained its electoral support up to 1933, and the Catholic population of Germany was under-represented among the supporters of the NSDAP at the polls, there was no possibility of its participation in a broad anti-Nazi coalition. Similarly, the prospects for political cooperation with the fourth leg of the republican coalition – the German People's Party (Deutsche Volkspartei, DVP) – were very slim. The immediate reason for the collapse of the coalition of SPD, Zentrum, DDP and DVP in March 1930 – the inability of the SPD and DVP to agree whether workers or employers should bear the burden of the rising costs of unemployment benefits – indicated the essential conflict of class interests which precluded broader political cooperation during a period of economic recession. The DVP had, in any case, moved sharply to the right following the death of Stresemann in October 1929; and, from the elections of September 1930 onwards, was to decline rapidly as a political force.[11]

The essential obstacle to any broad-based coalition against the rise of the authoritarian Right was thus the polarisation of politics which took place against the background of social and economic crisis after 1929/30. The policy of parliamentary 'toleration' extended towards the Brüning government by the SPD not only threatened to deprive it of its political rationale, as the policies for which it had struggled in the 1920s (especially the expansion and reform of state social welfare policies) were slowly reversed, but also widened the gulf between itself and the KPD whose supporters were particularly badly hit by welfare cuts and deflationary economic policies in general. On the other hand, as a consequence of the radicalisation of its members as the recession deepened, the SPD felt unable to participate in government and so was unable to modify the extent of the cuts.[12] For their part, the 'bourgeois' parties were to shift rightwards after 1929/30, not only as a consequence of the class interests of their supporters, but also in a (largely fruitless) attempt to prevent these from switching their alliance to the NSDAP, which increasingly presented itself to potential middle-class supporters as the only bulwark against a putative Bolshevik revolution.[13]

THE POLITICAL EXCLUSION OF THE LEFT IN 1933

When Hitler was appointed Chancellor in January 1933, the NSDAP had clearly failed to win the electoral support of a significant proportion of the German industrial working class. Yet the long-term foreign policy objectives of the Nazi leadership demanded the integration of the industrial working class into the 'national community' (*Volksgemeinschaft*). The Nazi leadership, especially Hitler himself, was paranoid about the possibility of victory in an imperialist war being undermined by a disloyal working class on the home front.[14] From the outset, then, the NSDAP in power was committed to the repression of the workers' movement and the destruction of working-class representative institutions – the SPD, KPD and the trade union movement. Yet the means by which this aim was to be achieved were by no means clear: rather, the regime was to be subjected to considerable pressures which helped to mould the form its policies assumed.[15] Foremost amongst these pressures were the activities of the party and paramilitary SA on the ground.

Following the *Reichstag* fire (27/28 February 1933), a wave of local party and SA activity against the Left began to force the regime's hand and led it to abandon its earlier tactic of only gradually escalating the political intimidation of the Left before the national elections of 5

March. The employment of the SA as auxiliary police in Prussia had, to some extent, already initiated this change of tactics, but the deployment of state and party power against the Left assumed a qualitatively different nature after 28 February. Hitler, Göring and Goebbels appear to have imagined quite genuinely that the burning of the *Reichstag* was a signal for a general communist uprising, and this belief led them to abandon their earlier plans of postponing the massive repression of the KPD until after the 5 March elections when, they had believed, they would be in a stronger position to deal with the party. On the basis of the Decree of the Reich President for the Protection of People and State, of 28 February, which suspended the basic civil liberties of the Weimar constitution, a full-scale terror campaign against the KPD was unleashed.[16] This terror campaign assumed the form of large-scale arrests of members of the KPD, the occupation of KPD offices and the elimination of the communist press. Thus, in the two weeks following the Decree of 28 February, perhaps 10 000 communists were arrested in Prussia alone. These arrests seem to have been concentrated on middle-ranking KPD functionaries although, as early as 3 March, Thälmann and the group of functionaries with him were captured in Berlin.[17] Although the KPD had long made preparations for the eventuality of its being forced underground, these proved ineffective, not least because any shift of the party organisation on to a clandestine footing could only be partial if the party was to continue to contest the 5 March elections.[18] Against the background of this terror, it is perhaps surprising that the number of votes cast for the KPD in the national elections fell by less than 20 per cent – from 5.9 million in November 1932 to 4.8 million in March 1933.[19] The mass arrests of communist leaders and functionaries had, however, paralysed the KPD for the time being.

The SPD also suffered serious harassment on the ground from the SA and police in the period leading up to and following the elections of 5 March; and the demoralisation that this caused among the membership of the SPD contributed to the passivity of the party leadership in the face of the Nazi 'seizure of power from below' in the regions (*Länder*).[20] This passivity was not, however, solely a consequence of the impact of Nazi terror and the impotence of the trade union movement in the face of record unemployment. The leadership was also hamstrung by an almost obsessive constitutionalism, which seemed to preclude mass illegal activity. This obsession with legality, which the SPD leadership hoped would preserve the organisational forms of the party, was – as has often been pointed out – in no small part a product of the 'organisational fetishism' which had developed in the party even before 1914.[21] But explanations of the passivity of the SPD leadership in 1932–33 which emphasise organisational conservatism should not blind us to the implications of the SPD's history as the party associated *par excellence* with the democratic constitution of Weimar after 1919. Advocacy of mass illegal activity may have seemed not only out of touch with social, economic and political reality, but also as being a negation of the SPD's image and role as a democratic republican party. In this context, it is important to remember that Hitler was appointed Chancellor quite legally.[22]

The SPD maintained its position of constitutional opposition to Nazism to the last – it was the only party in the *Reichstag* to vote against the Enabling Bill of 23 March, a measure which gave the Reich Chancellor powers to rule by decree.[23] But by this stage opposition to the new regime was becoming increasingly difficult. The SPD's property had been confiscated on 10 March and the social democratic press was suppressed. The occupation of the offices of the independent trade unions and the confiscation of their property on 2 May completed the destruction of the principal democratic opposition to the Nazi regime. In early May, SPD emigrés called for opposition to the new regime and this activity was used as a pretext to ban the SPD on 22 June. The Law against the Establishment of Parties of 14 July, outlawed all political parties other than the NSDAP.[24]

The reasons for the failure of a united Left opposition to Nazism to emerge before 1933 have been outlined above; as has the process whereby the Left was forcibly excluded from public political activity following Hitler's appointment as Chancellor. The obstacles in the way of a united anti-Nazi front on the left were formidable; perhaps insuperable. Yet, even had such an alliance emerged, it is difficult to see what kind of opposition to the Nazi seizure of power might have been successful. The SPD and KPD were increasingly isolated from 1930 onwards; and, though they retained their electoral bases in the face of Nazi appeals to the working class, the combined votes of the two parties of the Left amounted to barely more than a third of all votes cast in the elections of 1932. Granted the willingness of the Right and the Centre Party to tolerate a Nazi-led government, constitutional parliamentary opposition to the new regime was doomed to be fruitless. Even had the SPD been willing to cooperate with the KPD in organising a mass political strike, there is much evidence to suggest that this would have failed. Opposition, then, could only have taken the form of mass violent action. Here the constitutionalism of the SPD was crucial, and its failure to oppose by force the dismissal of the Prussian *Landtag* government by von Papen in July 1932 is sometimes seen as symptomatic of its fatalism in the face of an increasingly aggressive Right.[25] Yet there are good reasons for maintaining that the SPD pursued the only reasonable course of action open to it. Whilst many of the younger members of the *Reichsbanner* Defence Units – 200 000 strong in all – were keen to fight, they lacked military training and equipment and would almost certainly have been no match for the *Reichswehr* (possibly supported by the SA and the nationalist paramilitary organisation, the *Stahlhelm*). In any case, when von Papen dismissed the Prussian *Landtag*, the SPD in Prussia had been defeated at the polls.[26] The reluctance of the SPD leadership to launch a bloody civil war, in which they would be defending a minority government and in which the outcome seemed likely to be defeat, is perhaps understandable; and if the arguments for militant action seemed weak in the summer of 1932, they can have appeared no stronger in spring 1933 when support from the SA and the *Stahlhelm* for the army to oppose such action would have been a certainty. It has been pointed out that in 1934, the Austrian Left, which *was* united, was crushed by the army and conservative forces.[27] There is little reason to believe that mass violent opposition to the Right in Germany, either in 1932 or in 1933, would have been any more successful.

THE FAILURE OF RESISTANCE

The destruction of the political parties of the Left and of the trade unions in spring and early summer 1933 deprived German workers of representative institutions of their own choosing. Yet the destruction of these organisations, and the subsequent monopolisation of the public sphere by the Nazi regime, did not signal the transcendence of class conflict which Hitler and other Nazi leaders saw as an essential prerequisite for a war of imperial expansion. The Nazi regime was never to succeed in realising its conception of the *Volksgemeinschaft*, in which industrial workers subordinated their material interests to the demands of the rearmament, and later war, economy. Indeed, there is considerable evidence to suggest that, as full employment was achieved, industrial workers sought to exploit their scarcity value to improve their pay and working conditions in ways which may have hampered the concentration by the regime of Germany's human and material resources on rearmament and war.[28] Industrial workers were not won over to enthusiastic support of the regime after 1933 – indeed, the security organs of the regime were ever-vigilant for any signs of emerging working-class discontent – and, during the early years of the regime (1933–36), working-class discontent with the regime was marked.[29] On the other hand, this discontent with the regime never crystallised into overt resistance, and root and branch oppositional activity to the regime was confined to a small minority of (mainly communist) workers.[30] In practical political terms, therefore, the efforts of the SPD and KPD to organise resistance to the regime must be accounted to have been a failure: the regime was never threatened by working-class protest.

The two parties adopted markedly different strategies after 1933.[31] From the outset, the SPD had a much more pessimistic view of what could be achieved by underground activity within Germany. After an initial period of underground activity, the party came to acknowledge the dangers inherent in the attempt to maintain an active clandestine organisation in a police state. By 1935/36 at the latest, the party in exile (known as the *Sopade*) had abandoned any hope of mass discontent leading to the overthrow of the regime from within. By the later 1930s, the Gestapo was recording no or negligible underground activity by 'Marxists' (i.e. social democrats) in its monthly 'situation reports'. The party had come to see its role as one of attempting to hold together former members in informal meetings; and the leadership in exile – at first in Prague, later in Paris – increasingly looked to defeat in war as the only means whereby the regime could be overthrown.[32] The *Sopade* maintained a wide network of contacts within Germany and through these gathered information on social, economic and political developments, which it published in its so-called 'Germany Reports'.[33] The party in exile never underestimated the discontent which existed amongst broad sections of the German population, but emphasised the increasing disorientation, even of former party members, and the impossibility of effective active resistance in the face of a highly organised police state apparatus.[34]

The KPD, by contrast, never abandoned its belief in the possibility of active conspiratorial opposition to the regime. Such activity consisted principally of the printing and distribution of oppositional leaflets. The immense dangers which confronted the participants in such activity were increased by the pyramidal structure of the KPD underground. On numerous occasions the capture by the Gestapo of middle or high-ranking functionaries within the underground KPD organisation led to the arrest of dozens or even hundreds of ordinary underground workers. In 1935/36, in particular, the Gestapo was able to make mass arrests which did immense damage to the underground resistance.[35] In the later

1930s, the KPD was both to reorganise its underground units – in an attempt to contain the damage which followed the arrest of individual resistance members – and to place greater emphasis on the penetration of Nazi organisations such as the German Labour Front (the 'union' set up by the regime in May 1933 to replace the independent trade unions) by members of the resistance. The members were then to seek to use such organisations as a means of pressing workers' demands legally and so politicising working-class discontent with the regime. There is little evidence to suggest that this 'Trojan horse' strategy was any more successful than outright opposition to the regime had been; though it reduced the numbers of underground workers who were arrested by the Gestapo.[36]

Whilst the underground oppositional activity undertaken by the KPD in the years immediately following the Nazi seizure of power was characterised by the participation of a high proportion of the 1933 party membership – perhaps half of whom undertook some illegal political activity in the period 1933–35 – by the late 1930s the bulk of the former membership was resigned and inactive.[37] The outbreak of war in September 1939 did little to change this. The obligation felt by the KPD to defend the Ribbentrop–Molotov pact of August 1939, as a measure which contributed to the security of the Soviet Union, cut the ground from under the feet of the underground party; and only with the German invasion of the Soviet Union in June 1941 and the massive influx of foreign slave workers into Germany did underground communist activity take off again.[38] By this stage of the war, however, the existence of an ever-more autonomous and brutal terror apparatus and the increasing absorption of the German industrial workforce with the problems of day-to-day existence, sharply reduced any possibility of the open politicisation of workers' discontent.[39]

CONCLUSION

By any standards, the defeat suffered by the German labour movement in 1933 was enormous. Its origins, it is suggested here, lay not only in the deep political divisions within the German industrial working class before 1933, but also in the devastating impact of the Depression on the labour movement. The reaction of the Comintern to the defeat of continental Europe's most highly organised labour movement – and the only Communist Party outside the USSR with a mass membership – was tardy. The change introduced at the Seventh World Congress of the

Comintern in summer 1935 was to lead to the participation of communists in inter-class electoral pacts in France and Spain formed explicitly to resist the authoritarian Right, and, indeed, in Spain there followed participation in the government itself; but for the German working class it was too late.[40] The impact on the Nazi regime of communist resistance bore little relation to the enormity of the sacrifices made by rank-and-file communists between 1933 and 1945. Despite Hitler's fears, there was no repetition of November 1918. Democracy – and the German labour movement – was rebuilt after 1945 *from outside*.

Notes

1. J. Noakes and G. Pridham (eds) *Nazism 1919–1945. 1: The Rise to Power 1919–1934* (Exeter University Press, 1983), doc. 60, p. 83; Helmut Drüke *et al., Spaltung der Arbeiterbewegung und Faschismus. Sozialgeschichte der Weimarer Republik* (Hamburg, 1980) table A19, p. 196.
2. Timothy W. Mason, *Sozialpolitik im Dritten Reich. Arbeiterklasse und Volksgemeinschaft* (Opladen, 1977) pp. 42–69. Regional studies have emphasised the failure of the NSDAP to win the support of industrial workers before 1933. See, for example, Wilfried Böhnke, *Die NSDAP im Ruhrgebiet 1920–1933* (Bonn-Bad Godesberg, 1974).
3. Mason, *Sozialpolitik*, pp. 69–72.
4. Dick Geary, *European Labour Protest 1848–1939* (London, 1981) p. 168. On the general development of the KPD during the Weimar Republic see: Hermann Weber, *Die Wandlung des deutschen Kommunismus. Die Stalinisierung der KPD in der Weimarer Republik* (Frankfurt/Main, 1969); Siegfried Bahne, *Die KPD und das Ende von Weimar. Scheitern einer Politik* (Frankfurt/Main, 1976).
5. Bahne, *Die KPD*, pp., 29f.
6. Ibid., p. 23; Geary, *European Labour Protest*, pp. 168f.
7. Ibid., p. 169. On the ban of KPD-organised demonstrations, see: Eve Rosenhaft, 'Working-class Life and Working-class Politics: Communists, Nazis and the State in the Battle for the Street, Berlin 1928–1932', in R. J. Bessel and E. J. Feuchtwanger (eds), *Social Change and Political Development in Weimar Germany*, (London, 1981) pp. 207–40, here pp. 224ff. On the SPD during the Weimar Republic, see: R. N. Hunt, *German Social Democracy 1918–1933* (Chicago, 1970); W. L. Guttsman, *The German Social Democratic Party 1875–1933* (London, 1981); Hagen Schulze, 'Die SPD und der Staat von Weimar', in Michael Stürmer (ed.), *Die Weimarer Republik. Belagerte Civitas* (Königstein, 1980) p. 272–86; Hans Mommsen, 'Die Sozialdemokratie in der Defensive: Der Immobilismus der SPD und der Aufstieg des Nationalsozialismus', in. Hans Mommsen (ed.), *Sozialdemokratie zwischen Klassenbewegung und Volkspartei* (Frankfurt/Main,

1974); Erich Matthias, 'German Social Democracy in the Weimar Republic', in Anthony Nicholls and Erich Matthias (eds), *German Democracy and the Triumph of Hitler* (London, 1971) pp. 47–57; Heinrich August Winkler, 'Spielräume der Sozialdemokratie – Zur Rolle der SPD in Staat und Gesellschaft der Weimarer Republik', in Volker Rittenberger (ed.), *1933. Wie die Republik der Diktatur erlag* (Stuttgart, Berlin, Köln, Mainz, 1983) pp. 61–75.

8. Detlev Peukert, 'Zur Rolle des Arbeiterwiderstands im "Dritten Reich"', in Christoph Klessmann and Falk Pingel (eds), *Gegner des Nationalsozialismus* (Frankfurt/Main, 1980) pp. 73–90, here p. 78.

9. Mason, *Sozialpolitik*, pp. 89–98; Geary, *European Labour Protest*, pp. 170*f*; Sidney Pollard, 'The Trade Unions and the Depression of 1929–1933', in Hans Mommsen, Dietmar Petzina and Bernd Weisbrod (eds), *Industrielles System und politische Entwicklung in der Weimarer Republik* (Düsseldorf, 1974) pp. 237–48.

10. A. J. Nicholls, *Weimar and the Rise of Hitler* (London, 1968) pp. 135*f*. The standard work on party politics during the final years of the Weimar Republic and the triumph of National Socialism is Erich Matthias and Rudolf Morsey (eds), *Das Ende der Parteien 1933* (Düsseldorf, 1960), see Morsey's essay on the Zentrum, pp. 281–453. Rudolf Morsey, 'The Centre Party between the Fronts', in, *The Road to Dictatorship. Germany 1918–1933* (London, 1970) pp. 77–92, here pp. 77*ff*.

11. Nicholls, *Weimar and the Rise of Hitler*, pp. 138*f*. Hans-Hermann Hartwich, 'Parteien und Verbände in der Spätphase der Weimarer Republik – Wirtschaftskrise und Polarisierung', in Rittenberger (ed.), *1933*, pp. 76–97, here pp. 79*ff*, 83. See also, L. E. Jones, 'The dissolution of the bourgeois party system in the Weimar Republic', in Bessel and Feuchtwanger (eds), *Social Change and Political Development*, pp. 268–88.

12. Mason, *Sozialpolitik*, pp. 95*f*; Schulze, 'Die SPD und der Staat von Weimar', p. 278.

13. Jones 'The dissolution of the bourgeois party'. On Nazi electoral propaganda before 1933, see for example, Noakes and Pridham (eds), *Nazism 1919–1945*, pp. 70–81; J. Noakes, *The Nazi Party in Lower Saxony, 1921–1933* (Oxford, 1971); Ian Kershaw, 'Ideology, Propaganda and the Rise of the Nazi Party', in Peter D. Stachura (ed.), *The Nazi Machtergreifung* (London, 1983) pp. 162–81.

14. Mason, *Sozialpolitik*, pp. 15–41.

15. Ibid., pp. 81*ff*; Noakes and Pridham (eds), *Nazism 1919–1945*, pp. 123*f*.

16. Ibid., pp. 139–44; Martin Broszat, *Der Staat Hitlers. Grundlegung und Entwicklung seiner inneren Verfassung* (Munich, 1969) pp. 82–108.

17. Broszat, *Der Staat Hitlers*, pp. 101*f*.

18. Bahne, *Die KPD*, p. 41.

19. Broszat, *Der Staat Hitlers*, p. 106.

20. Noakes and Pridham (eds), *Nazism 1919–1945*, pp. 138*f*. gives examples of letters of resignation from SPD members. On the seizure of power at the regional level, see Broszat, *Der Staat Hitlers*, pp. 108*ff*, 130–40.

21. Geary, *European Labour Protest*, p. 170; Schulze, 'Die SPD und der Staat von Weimar', pp. 280*ff*.

22. Erich Matthias, 'Die Sozialdemokratische Partei Deutschlands', in Matth-

ias and Morsey (eds) *Das Ende der Parteien 1933*, pp. 101–278.

23. Ibid., pp. 166*f*; Noakes and Pridham (eds), *Nazism 1919–1945*, pp. 159*ff*; Broszat, *Der Staat Hitlers*, pp. 108–17.

24. The text is reproduced in Noakes and Pridham (eds) *Nazism 1919–1945*, p. 167. On the demise of the SPD see Matthias in Matthias and Morsey (eds), *Das Ende der Parteien 1933*, p. 181. Mason, *Sozialpolitik*, pp. 82*ff* describes the impact of the Nazi terror campaign on the unions on the ground.

25. Erich Matthias, 'Social Democracy and the Power in the State', in *The Road to Dictatorship. Germany 1918–1933*, pp. 59–73, here pp. 68*f*.

26. Nicholls, *Weimar and the Rise of Hitler*, p. 162. The total membership of the *Reichsbanner* was perhaps 3.5 million, but the majority of these were unarmed and could have been deployed only if weapons could have been procured. Hunt, *German Social Democracy*, p. 52.

27. Geary, *European Labour Protest*, p. 170; Winkler, 'Spielräume', in Rittenberger (ed.), *1933*, pp. 72*f*.

28. This is the essential argument of Mason, *Sozialpolitik*. See also, Tim Mason, 'The Workers' Opposition in Nazi Germany', in *History Workshop Journal*, vol. 11 (Spring 1981) pp. 120–37.

29. Ian Kershaw, *Popular Opinion and Political Dissent in the Third Reich: Bavaria 1933–1945* (Oxford, 1983) pp. 72–95; Detlev Peukert, *Die KPD im Widerstand. Verfolgung und Untergrundarbeit an Rhein und Ruhr 1933 bis 1945* (Wuppertal, 1980) pp. 204–18.

30. The 'containment' of working-class discontent in Nazi Germany is explored in Tim Mason, 'Die Bändigung der Arbeiterklasse im nationalsozialistischen Deutschland. Eine Einleitung', in Carola Sachse *et al., Angst, Belohnung, Zucht und Ordnung. Herrschaftsmechanismen im Nationalsozialismus* (Opladen, 1982) pp. 11–53.

31. On the two parties after 1933, see Peukert, *Die KPD im Widerstand*; Horst Duhnke, *Die KPD von 1933–1945* (Köln, 1971); Hermann Weber, 'Die KPD in der Illegalität', in Richard Löwenthal and Patrik von zur Mühlen (eds), *Widerstand und Verweigerung in Deutschland 1933 bis 1945* (Berlin/Bonn, 1982) pp. 83–101; Patrik von zur Mühlen, 'Sozialdemokraten gegen Hitler', in ibid., pp. 57–75.

32. Detlev Peukert, 'Der deutsche Arbeiterwiderstand 1933–1945', in Karl-Dietrich Bracher, Manfred Funke and Hans-Adolf Jacobsen (eds), *Nationalsozialistische Diktatur 1933–1945. Eine Bilanz* (Bonn, 1983) pp. 633–54, here pp. 639*f*.

33. The 'Germany Reports' of the SPD in exile have recently been republished: Klaus Behnken (ed.), *Deutschland-Berichte der Sozialdemokratischen Partei Deutschlands (SoPaDe) 1934–1940*, seven volumes (Frankfurt/Main, 1980).

34. Kershaw, *Popular Opinion*, pp. 105–10.

35. Peukert, 'Der deutsche Arbeiterwiderstand', pp. 642*ff*; Peukert, *Die KPD im Widerstand*, pp. 116–93; Gunther Plum, 'Die Arbeiterbewegung während der nationalsozialistischen Herrschaft', in Jürgen Reulecke (ed.), *Arbeiterbewegung an Rhein und Ruhr. Beiträge zur Geschichte der Arbeiterbewegung in Rheinland-Westfalen* (Wuppertal, 1974) pp. 355–83, here pp. 371–8; Duhnke, *Die KPD von 1933–1945*, pp. 199*ff*.

36. Duhnke, *Die KPD von 1933–1945*, pp. 189–94, 205–209; Peukert *Die KPD im Widerstand* pp. 311–322.
37. Peukert, 'Der deutsche Arbeiterwiderstand', pp. 642*ff*.
38. Ibid., p. 644; Peukert, *Die KPD im Widerstand*, pp. 326–417; Plum, 'Die Arbeiterbewegung', pp. 378*f.*
39. Peukert, *Die KPD im Widerstand*, pp. 382–8; Wolfgang Franz Werner, '*Bleib Ubrig!*'. *Deutsche Arbeiter in der nationalsozialistischen Kriegswirtschaft* (Düsseldorf, 1983).
40. E. H. Carr, *The End of Comintern 1930–1935* (London, 1982) charts changes in Comintern policy. See also the review of Carr's work by Helmut Gruber in *New German Critique* vol. 30 (Fall 1983) pp. 195–200.

3 The Austrian Left and the Popular Front

Martin Kitchen

Although the Austrian Social Democratic Party tried everything possible to preserve party unity from the day of its founding congress at Hainfeld on New Year's Eve of 1889, this delicate balancing act had ceased to be effective by the final stages of the First World War as the Dual Monarchy began to fall apart and the question of 'reform or revolution', which had plagued the party for so long, no longer seemed to be purely theoretical. In the pre-war years the party had grown steadily, its influence had increased, and some modest reforms were secured. The theoretical works of Karl Kautsky, Rudolf Hilferding and Otto Bauer brilliantly articulated the dominant ideology of the Second International, and these key texts of what the American socialist Louis B. Boudin was to call 'Austro-Marxism' were widely admired as offering a satisfactory middle way between the reformist abandonment of Marxism by Bernstein and the revisionists, and the revolutionary radicalism of Lenin or Rosa Luxemburg.

Critics of the Austro-Marxists argued that either they were providing elaborate pseudo-radical justifications for timid reformist practice, or they were trapped in an outmoded and discredited ideology that was no longer able to explain the realities of contemporary capitalism. The Austro-Marxists tended to place their faith in the inexorable laws of historical development which would result inevitably in socialism, almost without human intervention. To the Left, such passivity was a betrayal of the revolutionary mission of the working class. To the Right, their Marxist rhetoric was outmoded and overly radical. In the pre-war years, however, it remained possible to maintain a somewhat precarious party unity by combining radical language with reformist practice, and to stop the party disintegrating into the countless warring factions which existed before Hainfeld.[1]

Although the party had enthusiastically supported the resolutions passed by the 1907 and 1912 congresses of the Second International against an imperialist war – the party press hammering home this message over and over again – and, in spite of the fact that there was a sizeable pacifist faction within the party, the party leadership endorsed the war as a justifiable struggle against Russian aggression and Tsarist tyranny. This caused no little dismay among the rank-and-file, who were bewildered by what appeared to be a complete reversal of previous policy. The Austrian working class on the whole did not share the bellicose chauvinism of the leadership, and although Viktor Adler, the party leader, tried to restrain his more outspoken colleagues, there was widespread disillusionment and many workers left the party and the trades unions. In Vienna and Lower Austria, the heartland of the party, membership fell by some 65 per cent between 1914 and 1916 and only began to pick up again when the party became more critical of the government's war policy.[2]

Left-wing opposition to the party leadership's wartime policy was slow to develop and was at first confined to a relatively small but highly articulate group which included Otto Bauer, Julius Deutsch, Robert Danneberg and Viktor Adler's son Friedrich. On 21 October 1916, in an act of desperation caused by his political and emotional frustrations, Friedrich Adler assassinated the Minister President Stürgkh. He immediately became a popular hero and his rousing speech at his trial, in which he denounced both the policies of the ruling class and the 'social patriotism' of the social democrats, met with an enthusiastic response. The murder was, for Friedrich Adler, a protest against the entire system, which included the party headed by his own father, prompting one historian to speak of 'patricide by proxy'.[3]

The murder of Stürgkh had the effect of making the left opposition seem more determined and more influential than they were in reality. According to Julius Braunthal, there were only about 120 members of the group in 1915–16 and they had no desire to break up the party.[4] Rather, they saw the party's support of the wartime political truce as an aberration that would soon be corrected. Victor Adler for his part tried desperately to mediate between the majority of the party and the left wing in the traditional manner of an Austro-Marxist. The Left were in no sense revolutionaries; they refused to agitate among the workers and did not actively challenge the party leadership. But within the left opposition there was a minute faction of radicals who followed a somewhat watered-down Leninist line and who had some influence among socialist youth organisations and school groups, and in the student associations. The Left were largely intellectuals, literati, students and schoolchildren who, feeling isolated both from the party leadership and from the working class, relapsed into a mood of frustration and resignation and failed even to attempt to build up mass support for their political position.

By 1917 the party was moving perceptibly to the left. The government felt obliged to make certain concessions in an attempt to reduce the mounting social tensions. The *Reichsrat* was reconvened. The social democrats wre permitted to send a delegation to the International Socialist Conference in Stockholm and to hold their first official conference during the war. The February Revolution in Russia gave further encouragement to the Left and demolished the argument that the war was a crusade against Tsarist despotism. Even President Wilson's high-minded utterances on the war provided some useful ammunition for the anti-war faction, and the Petrograd Soviet's call for an end to the war found a sympathetic echo in the Dual Monarchy.

The party conference was held in October 1917, and Otto Bauer, who had recently been released from a Russian prisoner of war camp, made a powerful speech in which he attacked the party leadership for its chauvinism and its reformism, but at the same time insisted that party unity had to be preserved. This 'declaration of the Left' was designed to avoid the split that had occurred within the German party and did much to counteract the effects of the leftward movement of the party in the months before the congress. Otto Bauer, who now emerged as the 'Crown Prince' of the party, thus did much to keep the party together with a new version of the traditional Austro-Marxist compromise. The Left provided the radical rhetoric, which served to keep the discontented within the party by making it seem far more revolutionary than it was in practice. The party was thus able to continue the balancing act between revolutionary rhetoric and reformist practice which had characterised it since the Hainfeld compromise.[5]

The apparent leftward movement of the party met with an almost immediate response. Party membership increased rapidly and workers returned to the unions, even though they never quite reached the 1913 figures. Bauer's denunciation of the war, his reaffirmation of the International's resolutions against war, and his attacks on the party leadership did much to keep the Left inside a party which appeared to be the most radical Social Democratic Party in Europe. Meanwhile, the trade union movement became increasingly militant. There were a number of important strikes throughout 1917, culminating in the mass strike of 14 to 22 January 1918, in which nearly a million workers were involved. The strike was not directed only against the material hardships of the worst winter of the war; the strikers also demanded an immediate end to the war on all fronts. The party tried to persuade the workers to return to work and to accept the modest concessions which the government was prepared to make. This caused considerable ill-feeling among the militant workers, but the majority of radicals still remained within the party fold, and many of those who might have been tempted to leave were arrested, often to the considerable relief of the party leadership. A very small group, however, decided to make the break and on 3 November 1918 the Communist Party of Austria (KPÖ) was founded.

More than anything else, the party was a gesture of protest directed at the social democrats. It was not an organisation of determined revolutionary Marxists. Its leaders had little political experience and virtually no following among the working class. The proclamation of a Soviet republic in Hungary resulted in a spectacular growth in membership – to 40 000 by June 1919 – but the social democrats proclaimed their solidarity with the Hungarians, thus preventing a mass exodus to the communists. The disastrously mismanaged coup attempt by the KPÖ on 15 June 1919 further discredited the party, and with the collapse of the Hungarian Republic on 1 August, there were few who still believed that Soviet power was a viable option for Austria. The party now relapsed into ultra-left sectarianism, attempting to make a virtue of its miniscule following by talk of a 'revolutionary minority' and by refusing to take part in elections. By the time of the Third Party Congress in 1919 the communists were of virtually no consequence in Austrian politics.[6]

As the Dual Monarchy began to fall apart in the autumn of 1918, only the Social Democratic Party gave any serious thought to the question of post-war policy. They decided that they would support a coalition government with the bourgeois parties and would proclaim a republic that would work for *Anschluss* with Germany. Since the German–Austrian state was thus seen as provisional, merely awaiting absorption into a greater Germany, it was felt that the old National Assembly which had been elected before the war should still be recognised as a legitimate representative body. The communists were virtually alone in condemning the *Anschluss* policy, but although this was a realistic view given the attitude of the Entente, it had almost no support. The monarchy collapsed and the republic was created, not because of the policies of the social democrats, but because of a long process of internal decay. Historians still debate whether the situation in Austria in 1918–19 was potentially a revolutionary one, but there will probably never be a definitive answer to this question. Of one thing, however, there can be little doubt – the social democrats actively restrained all revolutionary movements.

The party leadership was able to produce powerful arguments in its efforts to restrain the Left. A revolution in Austria would provoke the intervention of the Entente; therefore Austrian socialists should wait for the revolution to spread to England and France. Since Austria would soon become part of a Germany dominated by the Workers' and Soldiers' Councils, there was no need to go through all the misery of a revolutionary upheaval. Extensive nationalisation was rejected on the grounds that there was no point in nationalising the debts of bankrupt industries. Along with this 'wait and see' attitude went a commendable concern with immediate measures of social reform. Unemployment benefits were introduced in November 1918, and an eight-hour day was introduced the following month. Shortly afterwards, workers' councils were created which were designed to pave the way for a degree of workers' control in industry and the eventual nationalisation of key sectors. Such innovations were very popular and did much to placate the working class whose radicalism was also assuaged by rousing speeches in favour of the Soviet regimes in Budapest and Munich. There was also much talk of the objective situation being such that similar experiments in direct democracy were singularly inappropriate for Austria. In personal terms, Friedrich Adler's refusal to join the Communist Party on his release from jail and his return to the social democratic fold did much to convince the more militant workers to remain faithful to the party.[7]

Turning its back on experiments with alternative forms of political organisation, the party under the leadership of Renner – the leading spokesman of the right wing – promptly formed a coalition with the Christian Social Party and the Greater German Party. This coalition was maintained after the elections of 16 February 1919, when the Social Democratic Party gained 40.7 per cent of the vote and 72 seats, the Christian Socials, 69 seats, and the Greater Germans, 36. The right-wing parties badly needed the social democrats to control and restrain the radical demands of the demobilised soldiers, the unemployed and the militant workers. The party leadership was ready to oblige, for it opposed any suggestion of a revolution, but skilfully used the anxieties of the Right to push through a comprehensive reform programme. The party was able to force their bourgeois coalition partners to make concessions that were greater than those made in any other capitalist country at the end of the war because there was such widespread fear that, if these concessions were not made, the country would fall prey to the Bolsheviks. Thus, the party was also able to convince their radical followers to moderate their demands and to opt for reform rather than revolution by pointing out the very real achievements of the reform programme. The classic Austro-Marxist policy of compromise was thus ideally suited to the political situation – that is, if a revolution was to be avoided and social stability restored. The degree of the compromise can best be seen in the measures taken towards nationalisation. A law was drawn up which examined the possibility of nationalising coal and the railways, the iron industry, and lumber, but it was a declaration of intent rather than a carefully worked out policy. It placated the radical workers without unduly upsetting the bourgeois parties. After the collapse of the Hungarian Soviet Republic the issue of nationalisation was scarcely discussed, and when the coalition dissolved in 1920, it disappeared from the political agenda.[8]

The communist demand for 'all power to the Soviets' hardly gave cause for alarm because the social democrats effectively controlled the councils. Initially, these councils were not without influence. In the first months after the war they had controlled prices, provided social assistance, and in many instances saved poeple from starvation. In the elections for workers' councils in Vienna in 1919 the communists were only able to gain 5 per cent of the vote. As the new coalition government strengthened its position, the councils concerned themselves less and less with political issues; divesting themselves of their radicalism, they became strictly economic organisations which worked closely with the trade unions. They were no longer seen as the nuclei of a new socialist society, but rather as an effective means of securing much needed reform within a healthy capitalist society. Thus, the potential agencies of revolution promoted compromise and reform.

In June 1920 the coalition government fell and the social democrats reverted to their traditional role as an opposition party. This gave them the appearance of being far more radical than they were in fact, and the reversion was warmly supported by the rank-and-file, who had begun to feel increasingly uneasy about the alliance with the bourgeois parties. It was with great relief that loyal social democrats were once again, with good conscience, able to denounce the Christian Social Party as an agent of the imperialist bourgeoisie and traitors to the Austrian cause. Yet even so, the party refused to move too far to the left. It did denounce the Geneva Treaty of 1922, under the terms of which the League of Nations made a massive loan to Austria in return for far-reaching control over the Austrian economy which included drastic economy measures, a value-added tax, and the undoing of many of the achievements of 1918–19. Yet although the social democrats produced an imaginative plan of economic recovery which did not rely on outside resources, in the event the party abstained from voting on the treaty, thus enabling Ignaz Seipel's Christian Social Party to secure the necessary two thirds majority for ratification. There was much truth in Seipel's jibe that Otto Bauer was a man with two left hands, for his policy of neither one thing nor the other was calculated to alienate both the Left and the Right.[9]

The Communist Party was outspoken in its opposition to the Geneva Treaty, and its intransigent stand won it some new supporters. In July and August 1923 some gains were made in the elections to the factory councils, but these were lost in the parliamentary elections in September when the party steered an ultra-left course, denouncing any consideration of a coalition government and calling for the immediate creation of a workers' and peasants' state. Such a programme held no attraction for a working class which still remained loyal to the social democrats. Only within the trade union movement and in the army were the communists able to score any real successes. In 1921 they won 21 per cent of the votes for the soldiers' councils, and their newspaper, the *Red Soldier*, had a circulation of 4000.[10] The War Minister, Vaugoin, set about purging the army of communists and social democrats and was able to undo much of this work, although it proved to be a somewhat more difficult task than he had at first imagined. The communists also formed a 'Red Trade Union Opposition' in 1923 which had some impact, and their newspapers were increasingly influential. Thereafter, as the economy stabilised, the party declined and came dangerously close to falling apart as a result of endless sectarian squabbles.

The social democrats were no more able than the communists to exploit to their own advantage the widespread discontent at the disastrous economic effects of the Geneva Treaty. Their share of the vote in the 1923 elections went up, but the Christian Social Party remained in power. Their efforts were now devoted almost exclusively to improving and extending the social services in Vienna. The city council, dominated by the social democrats, introduced redistributive taxation, built impressive workers' housing, and the schools, hospitals and welfare services were the most impressive in Europe. 'Red Vienna' became a place of pilgrimage for socialists and was regarded with horror and alarm by the Right. Socialists saw the social services of Vienna as a 'partial realisation of socialism within the womb of bourgeois society', whereas the bourgeois parties denounced such expenditure as 'taxation sadism' and 'council house Bolshevism'.[11] The Right was determined to destroy this socialist bastion and the social democrats were equally determined to defend it, but they were forced increasingly on to the defensive, narrowing their political perspective from the national to the municipal and relying on the achievements of Red Vienna as an excuse for inaction elsewhere.

As support for the party gradually dwindled, in large part because of the stabilisation of the economy in the years before the Depression, a typically Austro-Marxist attempt was made to recover this lost ground. At the party conference at Linz in 1926, a new programme was produced which was the most radical and outspoken of any Social Democratic Party. The Austrian bourgeoisie was warned that should they attempt to frustrate the democratic transition from capitalism to socialism 'the working class would be forced to smash the opposition of the bourgeoisie by means of dictatorship'. Although this was little more than an expression of the party's intention to defend the constitution of the Republic against right-wing violence, it served in part to placate the radicals within the party, who were angry with the leadership for its passivity in the face of a series of violent attacks against members by right-wing extremists, and who also felt that more should be done to ensure that the working class received its fair share of the relative prosperity of the late 1920s. The Right, however, made considerable political capital out of the ominous word 'dictatorship' and painted the social democrats as the worst and most violent species of Bolshevik. The right wing of the party was delighted when Otto Bauer announced that 51 per cent of the vote was all that was needed to achieve socialism. Once again it seemed that the Austro-Marxist balancing act had worked its magic.

Ignaz Seipel attempted to exploit the rhetoric of the Linz programme to forge a 'bourgeois bloc', but although he had some success in winning the support of a number of right-wing malcontents, including monarchists and Nazis, the social democrats did exceptionally well in the elections of 21 April 1927, winning 42 per cent of the popular vote and 71 seats, while Seipel's bloc won 85 seats, obliging him to form a coalition with the *Landbund* (Agrarian League). The elections were held at a time when emotions were running high after the murder of a small boy and an invalid during a clash between fascist war veterans and social democrats in Schattendorf in the Burgenland. The murderers were tried and acquitted, and on 15 July a massive spontaneous demonstration took place outside the Palace of Justice in Vienna to protest against what was widely felt to be a crass example of class injustice. Armed police attacked the crowd, leaving 86 dead and 1100 wounded. The leadership of the party was taken completely by surprise by these events; it had not organised the demonstration, had proved incapable of controlling the crowds and was equally unable to exploit this dramatic and tragic event to its own political advantage. The Palace of Justice affair showed that, for all the radical phraseology of the Linz programme, the leadership was losing touch with the rank-and-file. The radical Right was thus given fresh encouragement, and on the eve of the Depression the working class had little confidence in their political leaders and were becoming increasingly fatalistic and demoralised.[12]

The Communist Party fared no better. The party lost votes in the elections of 1923 which triggered off a series of acrimonious debates between the various factions within the party. The right wing argued for a close association with the social democrats, whose fortunes seemed to be rising, but this was condemned by the left wing as craven capitulation. According to the left-wing analysis, what was needed was a determined revolutionary policy that brooked no compromise with the bourgeois state. Divisions between these factions became so intense that at the party conference in 1924 fights broke out, and the Communist International felt obliged to impose a new leadership on the party in an attempt to put an end to the factionalism. At the end of the year, Johann Koplenig was elected party leader at an extraordinary conference, and he did much to bring some sense of unity to the party, although the old factional fights continued to erupt from time to time.

After the Schattendorf murders the communists suggested forming a common front against fascism with the social democrats and promised that they would support social democratic candidates at the April elections. This offer was turned down by Otto Bauer, who blandly announced that as the party was 90 per cent Bolshevik, and as there was not the slightest danger of fascism, there was no point in such an alliance. After 15 July the communists decided to put the radical wording of the Linz programme to the test and called for the arming of the working class to defend the Republic against the fascists, but the social democrats rejected this out of hand by saying that it would precipitate a civil war, alienate the rural communities – which they were trying to win over by means of an agricultural programme published in 1925 – and lead to serious economic disruption.[13]

The social democrats were irresolute in the face of the growing challenge from the Right and their radical rhetoric wore increasingly thin, but the communists were incapable of providing a viable alternative strategy. All too easily they lapsed into empty revolutionary jargon which reflected an almost total lack of understanding of the political realities of the day, and they remained a small sect with virtually no followers. In 1930 when the Austrian Nazis got more than 110 000 votes in the national elections, the communists won just over 20 000. The increase of 73 per cent in party membership in 1930 appears far less impressive when expressed in real terms. It rose from 1500 to 2600, which hardly compares very favourably with the social democrats' membership for 1930 of 600 000.[14]

With the onset of the Depression, extremist demands for the destruction of 'Red Vienna' and for an authoritarian regime became increasingly strident, and the social democrats started negotiations with the government which resulted in a strengthening of the executive powers of the president and a corresponding weakening of parliament. The party was able to derive some satisfaction from the fact that the extreme demands of the *Heimwehr* had been beaten back, but they were blind to the threat to their own position inherent in the exceptional emergency powers granted to the president.[15] Further successes in the elections of 1930, the last elections to be held during the lifetime of the Republic, strengthened the illusion that a significant victory had been secured against the fascists. In the summer of the following year Seipel made overtures to the social democrats, suggesting a possible coalition. This move was seen as an attempt to associate the party with the severe austerity measures which the government had introduced to deal with the economic crisis, which had become even more severe after the failure of the *Creditanstalt*. As the government was not prepared to make any political concessions or to alter its policies to accommodate the social democrats, even the right wing of the party, led by Karl Renner, rejected these advances.

Slowly, the position of the party was being eroded as the government moved to the right. In 1931 a putsch attempt by the *Heimwehr* led by Dr Pfrimer failed, but its leaders escaped punishment, showing that the social democrats' faith in the non-partisan nature of the courts was seriously misplaced. In May 1932 a new government was formed under Dollfuss, which was determined to crush social democracy and to establish some form of authoritarian regime – and with the Viennese *Heimwehr* leader, Emil Fey, in the government as Secretary of State for Security, this seemed to be no idle threat. The communists responded to the passivity of the social democrats by denouncing the leadership as agents of the bourgeoisie and as social fascists, while at the same time inviting the rank-and-file to join in a united front against fascism. Given that the Communist Party was still a minute sect rent apart by 'right opportunism' and 'left sectarianism', in the words of the International, this policy was totally unrealistic and had no impact whatsoever.[16] In the face of the growing threat from the Dollfuss government, such struggles between the two parties of the Left only harmed them both and made it impossible to create a common front in order to defend the Republic.

Within a year of forming his government, Dollfuss had dismissed the National Assembly and begun to rule by the 'Wartime Emergency

Economic Law'. May Day celebrations were banned and the Communist Party outlawed. The Social Democratic Defence Organisation (*Schutzbund*) was declared illegal, and party buildings were frequently searched for weapons. Severe restrictions were placed on the socialist press, and the influential *Arbeiter Zeitung* was no longer allowed to circulate freely. In spite of rousing speeches in defence of democracy and the heroic words of the Linz programme, the party did little to counteract this steady erosion of democratic rights and even prepared to negotiate with Dollfuss, using the somewhat lame excuse that the last vestiges of constitutional liberties had to be defended and that Dollfuss was a lesser evil than those on the more extreme right. Many rank-and-file members grew increasingly impatient with this supine attitude and demanded action, only to be warned not to provoke the government and to prepare for the day when the party would rise up in defence of the Republic. The communists were equally inept, resorting to empty rhetorical denunciations of the wickedness of the social democratic leadership, issuing weighty judgements on inter-imperialist contradictions, and announcing the arrival of a truly revolutionary situation, in which the class-conscious masses would rise up and overthrow the bankrupt bourgeois state. The Right was not impressed by such talk and organised the Patriotic Front to unite all anti-socialist forces in an effort to crush the Left.

As the Dollfuss regime tightened its grip and with the party leadership apparently suffering from a fatal paralysis of the will, many social democrats began to feel that the time had come for the *Schutzbund* to fight in defence of the democratic state, and the party headquarters in Vienna were flooded with letters from groups and individuals throughout the country demanding action.[17] Many members of the *Schutzbund* were prepared to fight even before the government had banned their organisation and, although it is true that some of these radicals were simply looking for violence and excitement and later left the party to join the Nazis who seemed to have more use for their talents, there can be no question that the leadership failed to realise the degree to which the rank-and-file was becoming increasingly concerned that the Austrian party would repeat the mistakes of its German comrades and offer no serious opposition to the rise of fascism. Most Austrian socialists were determined that their country should not go the same way as Germany and were deeply concerned that the leadership of the party appeared to be doing so little to stop the relentless destruction of the democratic state. They felt that the party's policy of the lesser evil was mistaken, for it was precisely this policy which had helped to bring Hitler to power.

The party leadership pointed to Dollfuss' ban on the National Socialist Party in June of 1933 as proof that he was better than the Hitlerites, but it was widely believed that this was merely repeating the mistakes of the German socialists who had supported Brüning for the same reason when he had banned the SA and the SS. The militants in the party argued that Dollfuss' pronouncements on the need for an authoritarian state and his meeting with Mussolini at Riccione in August 1933 were ample proof that he was bent on creating his own brand of Austrian fascism and that he had to be stopped before it was too late.

It was, thus, at a time of growing tension between the leadership and the rank-and-file that a special party conference was held in Vienna between 14 and 16 October 1933. From the outset the conference was dominated by the left opposition, and there were a number of motions put forward to force the leadership into action. It was suggested that a general strike in defence of democracy should be called according to the provisions of the Linz programme. Others went further and demanded armed resistance to the authoritarianism of the Dollfuss government. There was much harsh criticism of the party's policy of supporting Dollfuss as the lesser evil, and general agreement was reached that the time for compromise had ended and that the Dollfuss regime had to be resisted in the most effective way possible. Such criticisms of the leadership were not confined to the left opposition. Many moderate socialists, among them Manfred Ackermann, the spokesman for the white-collar workers, condemned the 'wait and see' attitude of the party and called for a properly considered strategy to defend the Republic and an end to the policy of resigned fatalism.

It was left to Otto Bauer to attempt to restore the credibility of the leadership. His speech was a remarkable performance, but he was clutching at straws. Claiming that the fact that the *Landbund* was no longer in the government was a sign that the bourgeois camp was falling apart, he suggested that the party might be able to win over substantial sectors of the rural population and thus strengthen the anti-fascist front. To those who preached armed resistance to fascistic inroads into the democratic state, he quoted Engel's strictures in the 1895 edition of *The Civil War in France* to the effect that armed insurrection was almost impossible against a modern state. Bauer tried to argue that the demand for such a violent anti-fascist policy was in fact a disguised call for revolution, and that as such it was an example of the worst form of putschism, which was bound either to fail disastrously or to lead to an unsavoury dictatorship. He did, however, concede that there were four instances when the party would be duty bound to fight. If Vienna had its independent rights stripped away; if the independence of the trade unions was compromised; if there was a direct attack on the party itself; and, lastly, if there was an attempt to change the franchise and to alter the constitution.

Bauer was later to admit that this speech was a mistake and that he was attempting to excuse the party's past actions rather than work out a strategy for the future. On the one hand, he was saying that resistance against the government was virtually impossible; on the other, that under certain conditions such a struggle would have to be undertaken. Many delegations to the conference did not feel that Bauer's assurances were sufficient and there were a number of calls for an active and vigorous policy rather than a purely defensive and reactive stance. The old hero of the Left, Friedrich Adler, attempted to defend the fatalism of the leadership by attacking what he felt to be the equally fatalistic attitude of the Left which appeared to believe that fascism was inevitable. At the end of the day the leadership triumphed, but it was a hollow victory. The Left had done most of the talking and had won most of the debating points, but they were out-voted by the silent majority, who were faithful to the leadership and who feared any precipitous action. They were further pacified by the resolutions calling for the reconvening of parliament, an anti-inflationary policy, the restoration of the rights of assembly and association, an increase in unemployment benefits, the lifting of all restrictions on the press, and the outlawing of all fascist paramilitary organisations.[18]

Up until the conference it had been just about possible to discount the left opposition as a group of young hotheads. However, at the conference it became clear that the Left was articulating a discontent at the passivity of the party leadership which was felt by a broad spectrum of members from all over the country. This was coupled with a growing feeling that a united front with the communists was needed to meet the threat of fascism.[19] What had begun as a movement in the Social Democratic Youth *Jungfront* had thus begun to attract much wider support. Most of the left opposition preferred to stay within the party, but a number of militants joined the communists in the months before February 1934. This was unfortunate, for it helped to convince the communists that their policy of unmasking the villainy of the social democrats was the most effective way of meeting the threat of fascism. It took a bloody civil war to expose the folly of the policy of 'class against class' and the rhetoric of 'social fascism'.

The party leadership dismissed most of this as the empty rhetoric of misguided youth and, largely ignoring the threat which came from the

Dollfuss government, concentrated most of their attention on the Austrian Nazis whom they saw as a far greater threat. The Dollfuss government continued its attacks on the social democrats, banning meetings and demonstrations, destroying the workers' councils, and introducing a new budget which was not even presented to parliament. The social democrats felt unable to do anything to counter these moves, for it was widely felt within the party that, at a time of such economic dislocation, a general strike was a totally impractical weapon. The leadership continued to believe that for Dollfuss the main enemy was national socialism, and that should there be a direct confrontation between the Christian Social and the Social Democrat parties, the Nazis would be the real winners. This analysis was perfectly correct, the only problem being that Dollfuss foolishly believed the exact opposite. In his view, the destruction of social democracy would convince Austrian Nazis to change their allegiance and join his party. When Dollfuss banned all political meetings between 1 December and 15 January in his 'Christmas Truce' the social democrats felt that this was aimed largely at the Nazis and therefore welcomed the move.

When it became clear that the party was lukewarm about the resolutions taken at the extraordinary conference and was apparently unwilling or unable to do anything to halt the steady erosion of democratic freedoms, the party began to fall apart. There was a dramatic decline in party membership – by one third between the time that parliament was closed and March 1933.[20] This decline in membership made it easier for left opposition groups within the party to attack the leadership, whose support came from the ordinary rank-and-file. The two most important left-wing groups were the Trotskyite 'Revolutionary Opposition within the Social Democratic Party of German Austria' and the 'Social Democratic Left' whose position was very close to that of the Communist Party, although the communists were singularly scornful of its efforts.

The party leadership was far more concerned with the Trotskyites than with the left opposition. Their wild talk of proletarian revolution, and madcap schemes for blowing up the sewage system in Vienna in order to destroy public buildings, alarmed the party so much that they were taken far too seriously. They were, in fact, a very small group, poorly organised and possessed of no talented spokesmen. The left opposition grew in strength and importance after the extraordinary congress. Its major contention was that the reformist leadership of the party was a serious hindrance to any effective anti-fascist struggle, for it was in effect supporting the 'agents of Italian fascism' in the mistaken belief that it was fighting the greater evil of Nazism. The leadership called the spokesmen of the Left to Vienna and made earnest pleas for unity, warning that in the face of the danger of fascism, factionalism within the party would be a disaster.[21] The delegation, which included Ernst Fischer's brother Otto and Koloman Wallisch, agreed to moderate their opposition, but returned home disappointed and frustrated.

The right wing of the party made offers to support Dollfuss in his efforts to combat the influence of the Nazis, but all such overtures were rejected out of hand. The government insisted that these offers were insincere, that the help of the social democrats was not needed, and that they could not be trusted.[22] The 'Situation Reports' of the party secretariat revealed clearly that Dollfuss was intent on destroying democracy in Austria and was equally determined to destroy the organisations of the working class. In January 1934, even the leadership began to ask how it was possible for them to continue to support a government whose economic policies were disastrous, which was undermining workers' rights and threatening drastic constitutional changes. Dollfuss had no real reason to be concerned. The party had accepted defeat after defeat, and there was no indication that it would do much if its remaining freedoms were taken away.

At 7.00 a.m. on 12 February 1934, the police stormed the Hotel Schiff in Linz, arresting the social democrat militant Bernaschek and precipitating a civil war which lasted for three days. Social democrats and communists fought side by side against government forces, thus spontaneously creating the United Front which the Communist Party had been advocating. But this did not mean for a moment that the communists were prepared to stop their criticisms of the Social Democratic Party leadership. The Czech communist Gottwald wrote: 'The facts indisputably prove that the Austrian Social Democrats have brought the Austrian workers under the yoke of fascist dictatorship'. The Communist International proclaimed that the United Front should be used to destroy and discredit the Second International.[23] But there were also signs that the position of the communists was beginning to change. Illya Ehrenburg published a series of articles in *Izvestia* at the beginning of March, on the fighting of 12 February, which suggested that the crushing defeat of the Austrian socialists could not simply be attributed to the perfidy of the social democratic leadership. The articles had warm words of praise for the leadership of the left opposition, and although Ehrenburg mocked the 'pacifists, Tolstoyites and vegetarians' in the party, he avoided the crude analysis of the initial Soviet response.

In the same month, Dimitrov blamed the Austrian tragedy on the social democrats, who had failed to realise that the only possible way to halt fascism was through an armed revolution. He mocked Otto Bauer for giving his pamphlet on the events of 12 February the title 'The Uprising of the Austrian Workers' and saying that the pathetic showing of the *Schutzbund* was the result of the 'capitulationist and defeatist attitude' of the leadership. Dimitrov put forward the exceptionally un-Leninist argument that the Austrian workers should have cast aside their leaders in February, whereupon a new leadership would have spontaneously arisen in the heat of battle. This extraordinary revolutionary optimism gradually began to wane, so that by the time of the Communist Party congress, held in September 1934, personal abuse of the social democratic leadership was noticeably absent, although Koplenig pointed out that the heroic fight of the *Schutzbund* in February could in no sense be attributed to the leadership.

The Communist Party grew greatly in size, immediately after February, as many social democratic militants joined the party. This seemed to be a triumphant vindication of the policy of the United Front, and, predictably, the social democrats were in an acute state of disarray. Most of the social democrats who remained in Austria, prominent among them Renner and Seitz, insisted that any attempt to establish an underground party was bound to fail. However, a small group of militants refused to accept this argument and on 9 March 1934 founded an illegal party called the Revolutionary Socialist Party. As the title of their new party suggests, they had moved markedly to the left as a result of the experiences of February, although they insisted that they were the legitimate heirs of the old party. They believed that what they were pleased to call Austrian fascism could only be destroyed by revolutionary struggle, by capturing the state apparatus, and by the institution of a proletarian dictatorship. All this was hopelessly vague and idealistic, the result of wild dreams that Black February would be followed by a Red October, – a slogan based on wishful thinking rather than on an objective analysis of the situation in Austria.[24] Meanwhile, in Prague, Otto Bauer and Julius Deutsch organised the exiled social democrats with their Foreign Office of the Austrian Socialists and continued to publish the *Arbeiter Zeitung* and the theoretical journal *Der Kampf*.

The Revolutionary Socialist Party, believing that the events of February had destroyed all 'democratic and reformist illusions', favoured the closest possible relations with the communists. At the same time it kept in close touch with the Second International; even though critical of its policies, it was grateful for the generous help that was provided for the victims of the February fighting. The revolutionary socialists suggested that there should be at least a non-aggression pact between the Second and the Third Internationals. The secretary of the International, Friedrich Adler, who sympathised with the revolutionary socialists, agreed that it was a good thing to get rid of all illusions, whether democratic or revolutionary, socialist or reformist, but he was anxious lest the Revolutionary Socialist Party, in its revolutionary zeal, might forget its commitment to democracy; and he pointed out that a united front with the communists would remain problematic for as long as they continued to denounce the social democrats as 'social fascists'.[25]

The communists were not particularly impressed by these appeals for unity. On 20 February the party announced: 'The united front of the revolutionary class struggle must remain alive in all the struggles of the workers, it must be built into revolutionary unity within the Communist Party'.[26] The communists regarded the revolutionary socialists as 'pseudo-leftists' and felt that if they wished to show their commitment to revolutionary socialism they should join the party. But the communists gradually began to change their tactics. When they realised that the social democrats were not going to join the party *en masse*, and the International became somewhat more flexible in its approach to the United Front, they suggested that it should be formed not only 'from below' but also 'from above'. The revolutionary socialists were prepared to accept this offer, provided that the communists respected their desire to remain affiliated to the Socialist International. In July 1934 the two parties agreed to work together through an action committee and, after the murder of Dollfuss by the Nazis, they published a declaration, which was also signed by the *Schutzbund*, that they would never enter into any negotiations with the government – as some former social democrats were suggesting – and that their aim was to overthrow Austro-fascism and to establish a dictatorship of the proletariat.

For the time being it was very difficult to go beyond the rather limited activities of the action committee. Otto Bauer's suggestion for a 'new Hainfeld', to create a new socialist party in Austria which would win back those social democrats who had defected to the communists after February, was attractive neither to the communists nor to the revolutionary socialists, prompting Bauer to pursue his thoughts of an 'integral socialism' affiliated neither to the Socialist nor the Communist International. The communists could only conceive of a united revolutionary party as one identical to their own, and thus the only alteration which they would consider was a possible change of name; the new party would continue to be a member of the Comintern. The revolutionary socialists suspected that the communists were merely planning to absorb their membership and were determined to preserve their organisational autonomy. Party members were less certain and, in some districts, voted in favour of uniting with the communists. Whether they understood the Communist Party's terms is, however, open to some doubt.

The situation changed significantly after the Seventh Congress of the Comintern and Dimitrov's five points on the United Front. These included complete independence from the bourgeoisie, the formation of united action committees, full recognition of the need to break the domination of the bourgeoisie by revolutionary action and to create the dictatorship of the proletariat, a refusal to support an imperialist war, and the creation of a party based on the principles of democratic centralism. The revolutionary socialists only objected to the last of these points, which would have meant a break with the Socialist International – a step which, for all their criticism of that organisation, they were unwilling to take. They were in no great hurry to unite with the communists, for the latter had reaffirmed at their congress in September 1934 that they were not an anti-social democratic party and generously admitted that the main enemy was fascism and not the reformism of the Socialist International. At the Seventh Congress, Dimitrov rejected the whole social fascist thesis as a mistake and insisted that there was a real distinction between bourgeois democracy and fascism. But lest it be thought that the International's previous line had been false, it was underlined that the tactics had to change because the objective situation had changed, not because the Comintern had been steering a mistaken course. In spite of a spirited defence of the social democratic leadership against the ludicrous charge of treachery in February, brought by Ernst Fischer (who appears in the protocol as 'Comrade Wieden'), it was strongly implied that the social democrats could not be trusted, and that the essential point of the United Front was to make it easier for party members to join the Communist Party – a point also made by Stalin at the Fifteenth Party Congress of the CPSU. But with the admission of certain sectarian errors, and some kind words for both Otto Bauer and the revolutionary socialists, the way was open for a genuine Popular Front between the Austrian parties of the Left.

Koplenig commented on Dimitrov's speech on the anti-fascist struggle by complaining of the ideological ambiguities of the revolutionary socialists and their campaign against the *Schutzbund*, the Communist International and the Soviet Union, and by insisting that although they supported the idea of the United Front in theory, in practice, because of the divisions between Trotskyite and reformist elements among the leadership, they harmed rather than helped the cause. He repeated his view that the United Front was simply the first step towards organisational unity on the basis of a Marxist–Leninist party; in other words that the revolutionary socialists would have to break with the Socialist International and join the Comintern.

The revolutionary socialists regarded the Seventh Congress as a thoroughgoing condemnation of the previous policies of the Comintern, occasioned by a fundamental change in the foreign policy of the Soviet Union. They regarded this *volte-face* with a certain scepticism and reserve, and with considerably less enthusiasm than Otto Bauer, who felt it was a serious mistake to see the congress as yet another expedient manoeuvre by the Soviet Union.[27] Whereas Bauer believed that the Social Democratic Party should immediately begin serious negotiations for a United Front, the Revolutionary Socialist Party decided to wait and test the sincerity of the communists' proposals.

The rank-and-file of the Revolutionary Socialist Party did not share the leadership's reservations about the communists' change of heart and demanded action towards unity. In response to this criticism, the leadership published a brochure proposing an 'action alliance' with the communists to last for one year during which time neither party would attack the other, although it was pointed out that a Popular Front was probably not suitable for Austria. The communists welcomed this initiative, but suggested that it needed to include a programme for a Popular Front government which would replace the fascist dictatorship. Discussions between the two parties continued, but the revolutionary socialists were more concerned to placate the 'unity fanatics' in their own ranks than they were to get too close to the communists.[28] Prodded by Dimitrov, who warned against the dangers of sectarianism and left-wing illusions, the Communist Party continued to press for a Popular Front and spoke admiringly of the splendid example set by the French Left. At the end of May 1936, the Communist Party announced that it supported the idea of a 'democratic government of the people', made up of all anti-fascist elements, which would not attempt to overthrow capitalism and establish socialism, but which would enable the communists to persuade the masses 'not to stay at this level of development, but to march onwards towards socialism'.[29]

By the summer of 1936, the Austrian Communist Party was thus committed to the idea of the 'democratic republic', but this was very difficult for many of the rank-and-file to accept. For years they had been warned against the dangers of 'democratic illusions' and of the noxious influence of the 'social fascists', and this change of course was too much for many of them to swallow. The revolutionary socialists argued that the Popular Front could not work in Austria, because there were no petit bourgeois or peasant organisations that might be attracted by an alliance of the Left. They also believed that the only effective form of anti-fascism was the socialist struggle for the dictatorship of the proletariat. Even in Spain and France, the revolutionary socialists felt that it was still too early to decide whether the Popular Front tactic was correct. The Revolutionary Socialist Party was thus divided between the leadership, who felt that although there was much to be said for the Popular Front, it simply would not work in Austria, and those in the rank-and-file, who believed that the whole idea was mistaken. After the collapse of the Popular Front in France and the defeat of the republicans in Spain, this argument gained credibility, and the revolutionary socialists tended to adopt an unfortunately self-righteous attitude towards the communists, combined with self-conscious attempts to place themselves to the left of the Comintern. There was much truth in this position, but the failure to create a Popular Front in Austria – a country where social democrats and communists had fought together to defend the republic – doubtless contributed to the failure to offer any effective resistance to Hitler's triumphal march to Vienna. The only concrete results of the Popular Front in Austria were agreements on the wording of declarations on the anniversaries of 12 February and on resolutions of solidarity with the republicans in Spain.

A major contributory factor to this friction between the revolutionary socialists and the communists was the effect of the Moscow show trials. The revolutionary socialists saw the trials not as an example of the dictatorship of the proletariat in action, but rather as Stalin's bid for absolute control of the party and the state, and as the crushing of inner-party democracy. The communists reacted vehemently to such criticism, attacking the revolutionary socialists for breaking the United Front, for giving aid and comfort to the enemies of the Soviet Union, and for harbouring Trotskyites and crypto-fascists within their ranks. But at the same time, the communists made earnest appeals to the revolutionary socialists not to criticise the course of Soviet justice and to remain true to their professions of solidarity with the first land of the workers and peasants. All this was exceedingly hard for non-communists to swallow. Before the Seventh Congress they had been condemned as social fascists if they disagreed with Zinoviev; now, if they had any kind words for him, they were denounced as fascists dogs and Gestapo agents. Otto Bauer and the revolutionary socialists continued to urge support for the Soviet

Union, but felt it their duty to make friendly criticism whenever it was needed. The communists continued to believe that any criticism of the socialist motherland was a betrayal of socialism. The revolutionary socialists felt that the right-wing course in the Soviet Union, of which the onslaught against any sign of 'Trotskyism' in the show trials was an essential part, was a radical break with the revolutionary traditions of the Soviet state to which they felt themselves to be the heirs.

The failure of the Popular Front tactic in Austria raises the fundamental question of the relationship between democracy and communism which was one of the central concerns of Austro-Marxism. Whereas the Communist Party first believed that it was a question of Soviet power or nothing, and then abandoned all such hopes in a Popular Front policy which was a purely defensive strategy designed to preserve the bourgeois democratic state against the onslaught of fascism, the social democrats wrestled with the problem of combining socialism with democracy. Otto Bauer's idea of an 'integral socialism', which would combine the vision and determination of the Bolsheviks with the commitment to democracy of the reformists, was just such an attempt. Bauer's ideas had almost no effect at all in Austria at the time, although they were taken seriously in Moscow. The revolutionary socialists never bothered to discuss them.[30] The communists were so concerned about their defensive tactics that they had no time for discussions about the future of socialism. The outstanding representative of the Austro-Marxist tradition, and the man who had the most to offer to the era of the Popular Front, was thus an exile and without influence in his own country

Although Austro-Marxism has been denounced from the Left for its pseudo-revolutionary ideology which merely misled the proletariat, and from the Right for its dogmatism and lack of realism, it has had a considerable influence on the Left since the Twentieth Congress of the CPSU in 1956.[31] It is a curious paradox that it was precisely in the country where the tradition of a socialism of compromise between Left and Right was strongest, where communists and reformists had fought on the barricades together and had set an example which was to do much to inspire the idea of a Popular Front elsewhere, that the policies of the Seventh Congress of the Comintern were so singularly unsuccessful. There were two main reasons for this. Firstly, the crushing defeat of February 1934 was so difficult to accept that socialists tended either to resignation or to the entertainment of unrealistic hopes. Secondly, outside the labour movement there were virtually no possible allies for a genuine Popular Front, and bourgeois democracy had, in any case, been virtually destroyed. The experience of Austria showed once again the fatal consequences of fractionalism, divisiveness and intolerance on the Left. But by the time this was realised, it was already too late.

Notes

1. Norbert Leser, *Zwischen Reformismus und Bolschewismus. Der Austromarxismus als Theorie und Praxis* (Vienna, 1968); Louis B. Boudin, *The Theoretical System of Karl Marx in the Light of Recent Criticism* (Chicago, 1907); Hans Hautmann and Rudolf Kropf, *Die Österreichische Arbeiterbewegung vom Vormärz bis 1945* (Vienna, 1974); Norbert Leser, 'Der Austromarxismus als Strömung des marxistischen Zentrums', *VIII Linzer Konferenz der Historiker der Arbeiterbewegung* (Linz, 1972). Kautsky lived in Germany before Hainfield and Hilferding moved to Berlin in 1906, but their influence on the Austrian party was so great that it is quite justifiable to call them 'Austro-Marxists'.
2. Hautmann and Kropf, *Die Österreichische Arbeiterbewegung*, p. 118.
3. Adam Wandruszka in Heinrich Benedikt, *Geschichte der Republik Österreich* (Munich, 1954) p. 440.
4. Julius Braunthal, *Victor und Friedrich Adler. Zwei Generationen Arbeiterbewegung* (Vienna, 1965) p. 233.
5. Hans Hautmann, 'Die Kriegslinke in der Sozialdemokratischen Partei Österreichs zwischen 1914 und 1918', *Die Zukunft* no. 13/14, Vienna, July 1971.
6. Hans Hautmann, *Die Anfänge der linksradikalen Bewegung und der Kommunistischen Partei Deutschösterreichs 1916-1919* (Vienna, 1970); Friedl Fürnberg (ed.), *Geschichte der Kommunistischen partei Österreichs*, (Vienna 1977); Herbert Steiner, 'Die Kommunistische Partei Österreichs von 1918 bis 1933. Bibliographische Bemerkungen', *Marburger Abhandlungen zur Politischen Wissenschaft*, vol 11 (1968).
7. Hans Hautmann, *Die verlorene Räterepublik*, (Vienna, 1971) p. 78; F. L. Carsten, *Revolution in Central Europe 1918-1919*, (Berkeley, 1972) pp. 78-126, 238-46.
8. Kurt W. Rothschild, 'Wurzeln und Triebkräfte der Entwicklung der österreichischen Wirtschaftsstruktur', in W. Weber (ed.), *Österreichs Wirtschaftsstruktur gestern-heute-morgen*, vol. 1 (Berlin, 1961).
9. Leser, *Zwischen Reformismus und Bolschewismus*, p. 367.
10. Fürnberg (ed.) *Geschichte der Kommunistischen Partei*, p. 57.
11. Wandruszka in Benedikt, *Geschichte der Republik*, p. 461. See, Felix Czeike, 'Wirtschafts und Sozialpolitik der Gemeinde Wien in der Ersten Republik (1919-1934)', *Wiener Schriften*, vols 6 and 11 (Vienna, 1958/9) for a discussion of these social programmes.
12. On the Palace of Justice affair see *Die Ereignissse des 15 Juli 1927*, (Vienna, 1979).
13. Some have argued that the failure to arm the workers in 1927 was a

disastrous mistake which led directly to the defeat of February 1934. See, 'George Wieser' [Otto Leichter], *Ein Staat Stirbt. Österreich 1934–38* (Paris, 1938).

14. E. H. Carr, *Twilight of the Comintern*, (New York, 1982) p. 275.
15. Leser, *Zwischen Reformismus und Bolshewismus*, pp. 440–8.
16. Carr, *Twilight of the Comintern*, p. 276.
17. Vienna: Österreichisches Staatsarchiv, Allgemeines Verwaltungsarchiv (AVA), Sozialdemokratisches Parteiarchiv, Parteistellen 175a.
18. The protocol of the conference had to be shown to the State Secretary for Security in person, and no details could be published in the press, VGA Lode 16, Mappe 33.
19. AVA, Parteistellen 123, for a resolution in August 1933 from the 19th District of Vienna calling for a united front.
20. AVA, Zl. Pr. 1V–2606/1934, Karton 6.
21. AVA, Parteistellen 35. For the Trotskyite opposition see, AVA, Zl. Pr. 1V–2606/1934, Karton 6.
22. AVA Bundeskanzleramt Inneres, 4885.
23. Carr, *Twilight of the Comintern*, p. 278.
24. Walter Wisshaupt, *Wir kommen wieder! Eine Geschichte der Revolutionären Sozialisten Österreichs 1934–1938*, (Vienna, 1967).
25. Friedrich Adler's correspondence with the Revolutionary Socialist Party is in, Vienna: Haus-Hof-und Staatsarchiv, Neues Politisches Archiv (NPA) Fasz. 292.
26. Franz West, *Die Linke im Ständestaat Österreich: Revolutionäre Sozialisten und Kommunisten 1934-1938* (Vienna, 1978) p. 65.
27. Otto Bauer, 'Einheitskampf in der Weltpolitik', *Der Kampf*, October 1935.
28. Joseph Buttinger, *Das Ende der Massenpartei. Am Beispiel Österreichs* (Cologne, 1953) pp. 310 and 303.
29. West, *Die Linke im Ständestaat*, pp. 199–200.
30. Otto Bauer, *Zwischen zwei Weltkriegen*, (Bratislava, 1936). Peter Pelinka, *Erbe und Neubeginn: Die Revolutionären Sozialisten in Österreich 1934–1938* (Vienna, 1981) p. 179.
31. Illias Katsoulis, *Sozialismus und Staat: Demokratie, Revolution und Diktatur des Proletariats im Austromarxismus*, (Meisenheim am Glan, 1975) pp. 389–408.

4 The French Popular Front, 1936–37

David A. L. Levy

INTRODUCTION

When French people cast their minds back fifty years to the time of the Popular Front, their most vivid memories tend not to be of Léon Blum or of the first socialist-led government in French history, but rather of the strikes of May and June 1936 that accompanied Blum's election. The scale of the strikes alone would have been sufficient to make the time memorable. There were more strikes in the single month of June than there had been during the previous fifteen years. But the factory occupations which accompanied the strikes also contributed to the festive atmosphere for which June 1936 is remembered. There were often open days and concerts in the occupied factories and entire communities would go to lend their support, to give food to the strikers, or simply to enjoy themselves. If the atmosphere surrounding the strikes was quite novel, so were the results of the workers' action. Under both the impetus and the threat of the strikes, the newly elected Popular Front government reacted with unparliamentary haste. According to one reckoning, 133 laws were passed in a mere 73 days.[1] The changes included the introduction of paid holidays for workers, a forty-hour week, substantial wage rises and improved trade union rights. The right-wing fascist leagues were dissolved by decree. It seemed as though the working class had taken control of the destiny of the French nation. Within the factories, workers showed a new self-confidence, no longer fearing either their employers or the foremen. Trade unions were newly powerful and for the first time ever they faced a sympathetic government. Even the playgrounds of the rich were transformed during the summer of 1936 as workers, benefiting from their paid holidays, invaded the beaches and exclusive resorts, and rediscovered the French countryside.

It was a time of great optimism. Yet many of the hopes of 1936 were soon to be disappointed. Before long the dream of a Popular Front of Bread, Liberty, and Peace had turned sour. The wage rises granted after the strikes were eroded by inflation. The newly won trade union rights were clawed back as employers recovered their self-confidence. The

jubilant atmosphere which had characterised the June strikes gave way
to bitterness as industrial conflict continued in the face of opposition
from employers and government alike. In the political arena the mood of
optimism, of unity and expansion on the Left in 1936 gave way to one of
division and decline in 1937 and 1938. Meanwhile, the parties of the
Right and the far Right expanded dramatically and the majority in the
Chamber of Deputies shifted its support to governments that were
Popular Front in name only. Internationally, the results were no better.
The anti-fascist commitment of the French Popular Front produced
little concrete help at government level for the Spanish Republic.
Similarly, French anti-fascists stood by, helpless, as Germany built up
its war machine and imposed ever-escalating demands on its neighbours.
Confronted with the reality of fascist expansion, the anti-fascists of the
French Popular Front were unable to choose between their desire to
oppose fascist aggression and their equally strong desire to avoid
another war at all costs.

Thus, the disappointment that followed the initial optimism of the
Popular Front was profound, and over the last fifty years there have
been a great many attempts to explain the failure. One group of analyses
has focused on the strikes, seen by some as evidence of a 'révolution
manquée', betrayed by the parliamentary parties; and by others as proof
of communist disloyalty to Blum. Other explanations have concentrated
on the parliamentary arena and particularly on the fickleness of radical
support for the Popular Front. There have also been 'institutional
explanations' that have found fault with the political system of the Third
Republic which allowed the indirectly elected and conservative Senate to
check the will of the directly elected Chamber. The aim in this chapter is
not to prove or refute any of these all-embracing explanations of the
Popular Front's failure, but to try to cast light on the circumstances in
which the failure occurred. The intention is, first, to examine the
creation of the Popular Front and the very different ways in which the
participants understood its ideological bases – Republicanism, anti-
fascism, social and economic reform – and, second, to look at the
differing degrees of significance which they accorded the Popular Front
programme. Thereafter the Popular Front in power will be examined,
and the ways in which the June strikes and the Spanish Civil War put the
coalition under strain precisely at its weakest points. The chapter
concludes with an examination of how events from September 1936 to
the fall of Blum in June 1937 brought the tensions within the Popular
Front to the surface. Insofar as a general interpretation is offered, it is
one which focuses on Blum's failures of political judgement; the

misguided sense of loyalty that he felt to a programme to which the other participants were only weakly committed; and his failure to comprehend how, although in the short term the strikes of June 1936 strengthened his hand to push for the introduction of radical reforms, in the medium term they would destroy any chance of realising his previous hopes for national reconciliation.

THE CONSTRUCTION OF THE POPULAR FRONT

Republicanism

The Popular Front originated in response to the events of 6 February 1934. It was on that day that Colonel De La Rocque led his right-wing Croix de Feu organisation in a demonstration and march on the Chamber of Deputies which ended in a bloody and murderous riot. To many contemporaries it seemed that France had witnessed a home-grown attempt at a fascist style *coup d'état*. Fifteen people had been killed and more than two thousand injured, and in a Republic where governments came and went with tedious frequency, the ninety-fourth government, under the leadership of Edouard Daladier, scored a first by stepping down from office as a result of street violence.[2]

The riots swiftly produced a movement to defend the Republic. On 12 February the warring Socialist and Communist Parties and their trade union allies, the CGT and CGTU respectively, joined in a general strike and nationwide series of protest demonstrations which con-stituted the most successful example of working-class mobilisation seen for years. One feature of the demonstrations, which took many people by surprise, was the way in which, even though the day's events had not been jointly organised, in Paris the rival socialist and communist cortéges spontaneously joined together as workers and rediscovered their sense of unity in defence of the Republic in spite of the bitterness which had separated their parties since 1920.

For the socialists, the size of the working-class response to De La Rocque was both understandable and a cause for celebration. As Blum himself said: 'When the Republic is in danger the word republican changes its meaning. It regains its old significance, historic and heroic'.[3] But for the communists, the strength of the working-class response and the obvious desire for greater unity on the Left posed problems. On the one hand it was clear that a change of policy to take account of the new republican and anti-fascist sentiment in the working class could work to the party's advantage.[4] But on the other hand, almost since its creation in 1920, the PCF had deliberately set itself the goal of establishing a new type of 'Bolshevised' party, free of the dead weight of republican values and socialist reformism, and committed instead to defending the Soviet Union and to building a specifically working-class revolutionary movement in France.

There was no sign in February 1934 that the PCF was about to change its purist and sectarian line. On the very morning of 6 February, *L'Humanité*, the party newspaper, called on its readers to demonstrate 'at one and the same time against the fascist bands and against the government which protects them and helps create them, against social democracy which, by its division of the working class, attempts to weaken it'.[5] Appeals from Blum for the PCF to take part in the organisation of the 12 February counter-demonstration went unheeded. A week later, *L'Humanité* countered with a rejection of the very notion of republican defence: 'Defend the Republic says Blum? As if fascism was not an extension of the Republic, as if the Republic itself isn't the basis of fascism?'[6]

In time the PCF did change its line, becoming the most enthusiastic proponent of left unity and laying claim to be a super-republican party. Indeed the party itself became the moving force behind the Popular Front, providing both the political initiatives and the slogans for the movement.[7] But in the eyes of many socialists and Radicals, the timing of the PCF's policy change both revealed its origins as lying in Moscow and cast doubt on its sincerity.[8] The critics noted that from February to June the PCF had continued with its abuse of the socialists and members who had argued for greater cooperation between the parties had been excluded.[9] The change in PCF policy only came in June at the party's conference at Ivry. Fresh from a visit to Moscow and with a telegram of instructions recently arrived from the Comintern, Maurice Thorez, the party leader, used his closing speech to start the delicate process of reversing policy by calling for unity of action with socialist workers to be achieved 'at any price'.[10] The price which the socialists extracted was a non-aggression pact, signed between the two parties on 27 July 1934, before the PCF went on to launch the call for a vast 'rassemblement populaire' which would include the radicals, as well as socialists and communists.

It took a year of painstaking effort before the PCF's increasingly moderate posture succeeded in winning Radical Party support for the idea of the Popular Front, but when the Radicals finally responded to the call from the Comité de Rassemblement Populaire to take part in a mass meeting on Bastille Day, 14 July 1935, the result was a resounding success. The size of the demonstration which followed the meeting – 500 000 according to some reports – testified to the popularity of the Rassemblement Populaire, while its timing highlighted the importance that the old revolutionary and republican tradition would assume within the new movement. The call to the meeting included the pledge: 'on this day which reminds us of the first victory of the Republic, to defend the democratic liberties conquered by the people of France, to give to the workers bread, to the young people work, and to the world a great human peace'.[11] All the parties of the Left found the success of the meeting encouraging, but in different ways. The communists rejoiced at their success in winning the support of the Radical Party and its largely middle-class supporters for a movement against fascism, while the Radicals congratulated themselves on their success in winning over the far left to republicanism.[12] The meeting opened the way for the negotiations which led to the signing of the programme of the Rassemblement Populaire in January 1936, which in turn was followed by the reunification of the trade union movement in a single CGT in March 1936, and finally by the election victory of May of that year.

Belligerent versus Pacifist Anti-fascism

The reflex of republican defence was as old as the Republic itself. The novelty of the Popular Front lay in the way it succeeded in rejuvenating this traditional political response through the new threat of fascism. But if republicanism had always been an imprecise ideology, anti-fascism was little better. For some anti-fascism was little more than a revived republicanism with the difference only that this time the enemy, in the shape of De La Rocque and the far-right leagues, was dubbed 'fascist' in character. Other anti-fascists shared the fears about De La Rocque but were also concerned about the dangers posed by foreign fascism. In the international sphere, however, the communist commitment to what might be termed 'belligerent anti-fascism', based on firm resistance to Hitler, tended to clash with the pacifism which coloured the SFIO's anti-fascism.

Socialists recognised, and for the most part accepted, that the PCF's late rallying to the cause of left unity was probably linked as much to Moscow's fears of German expansion as it was to strictly domestic French concerns. And initially, since the PCF's anti-fascism was grafted on to its own tradition of vigorous anti-militarism, there was no direct clash with the socialists' emphasis on pacifism, disarmament and collective security. But when the signing of the Franco–Soviet pact in

May 1935 was accompanied by a communiqué which declared that Stalin approved of French efforts at rearmament, the clash became acute.[13] Within, twenty four hours the French communists had fallen into line, putting up posters declaring, 'Stalin is Right!' and disowning their previous fifteen years of anti-militarist campaigns. This about-turn opened the way for the party to embrace an internationally directed and belligerent anti-fascism which contrasted sharply with the domestically inspired, republican and pacifist anti-fascism favoured by the other Popular Front parties.

Stalin's endorsement of French military efforts disturbed many French socialists. Blum wrote of how socialists:

> have always denied that the security of a nation was dependent upon the strength of its armed forces. Now Stalin recognises that the security of France depends upon an increase in her military strength . . . Stalin approves, against us, of the government which we have fought.[14]

This commitment to disarmament meant that many party members were loathe to take seriously the threat posed by Hitler, and there was a great reluctance to even contemplate the idea that resistance to international fascism could ever conflict with the party's traditional commitment to pacifism.[15] A speaker at the February 1936 Socialist Party Congress revealed the thinking of a large section of the SFIO when he said, '. . . it will depend on us whether the inevitable expansion of Germany will be peaceful or warlike', adding, 'we do not intend to make anti-fascism into a doctrine of foreign policy; we do not want a war which tomorrow will aim at bringing freedom at gunpoint'.[16]

This pacifist-inspired view of the fascist threat put the SFIO in a very weak position thereafter, in terms of the resistance which it was able to offer to fascist aggression. Indeed, as the threat from foreign fascism increased, whether through Hitler's remilitarisation of the Rhineland in March 1936, through General Franco's revolt against the Spanish Republic in July of the same year, or through Germany's subsequent aggression against both Austria and Czechoslovakia, at each stage there were those in the SFIO who reacted by simply returning ever more determinedly to their pacifist heritage.[17]

The Working Class and the Third Estate

The confusion and contradictions which underlay the anti-fascist and republican bases of the Popular Front also applied to its conception of class. Once again there were real conflicts of interest and opinion between the Popular Front parties, and most particularly between the largely middle-class, economically conservative Radical Party and the two working-class parties, the Socialist and the Communist Parties. But in the interests of anti-fascist and republican unity these differences were either overlooked or played down, and the old eighteenth- and nineteenth-century themes of the 'Third Estate' against 'Reaction' and of 'le peuple' against 'les gros' were substituted for the language of class. Even the fight against fascism was presented as a campaign for the entire nation, with the fascist leagues presented as the tools of a financial oligarchy made up of the 'two hundred families' who, it was claimed, secretly controlled the destiny of France.[18]

Attacks on the two hundred families usually originated from the Radical Party but the new, moderate PCF leadership made the call for the union of the French people against the two hundred families the main theme of its election campaign.[19] Meanwhile, the Socialist Party Secretary, Paul Faure, was proclaiming that at last 'we must be rid of the oligarchy of a fistful of individuals who hold the nation to ransom, betray it at will, and oppress and enslave the mass of citizens'.[20] This kind of language served to create an impression of universality, excluding all but the Popular Front's supporters from what was effectively a redefinition of the national community as Third Estate. But while the rallying cries to defend the Republic against the fascists, the plutocrats and the two hundred families helped to create a mobilising and unifying myth for the Popular Front, they also tended to blind the coalition partners to the complexity of class relations and to the very real conflicts of class, interest and opinion which coexisted within their own ranks.

THE POPULAR FRONT PROGRAMME

The negotiations over the Popular Front programme reflected the ambiguity and contradictions of the coalition itself. All the parties assumed that in the event of electoral success it would be the moderate Radical Party which would lead any future Popular Front government. While the socialists saw the programme as an opportunity to put forward proposals for substantial structural reform, communist determination to retain radical support for the Popular Front led them to join with the radicals in blocking these moves. Communist moderation in the negotiations was so pronounced that it made the socialists look like 'intransigent sectarians'.[21]

The end result of these negotiations was a programme which was deliberately limited in scope so as to include only those measures which were immediately applicable. The political demands included measures for the defence of liberty – such as the banning of the fascist leagues – reform of the press, and a guarantee of secular education, together with the demand that the school-leaving age be raised to fourteen. Most of these measures fell in with traditional Radical Party concern for individual liberties. A second section of the programme dealt with the protection of peace, which mainly amounted to a defence of the League of Nations and of collective security, but it also included a call for the nationalisation of key war industries. In the economic sphere, the programme called for a reduction in the working week, a programme of public works, a restoration of farm prices and the creation of a National Wheat Office, the repeal of the deflationary laws of the Laval government, and financial reform.[22]

The programme was seriously limited by the fact that it did not commit its signatories to honour it either as an electoral or a governmental platform. The lack of commitment was most obvious among the radicals. Indeed, 70 per cent of those Radical Party deputies elected in 1936 shied away from even mentioning the existence of the Popular Front in their local manifestos. The only element of the Popular Front programme which received enthusiastic endorsement from Radical candidates was the proposal for the dissolution of the fascist leagues. In the economic sphere, a full third of the Radical deputies endorsed the deflationary policies of the previous government, while few of the others showed much enthusiasm for the reflationary economic measures contained in the Popular Front programme. In short, the election campaign showed that although Radical candidates were formally linked to the Popular Front they were 'in reality very divided, unsure of which economic or social policy to pursue and in many cases, terrified of the adventure' which the Popular Front represented for them.[23]

Radical doubts about the Popular Front were increased rather than diminished by the election result. Although the elections produced a Popular Front victory, this was not the result of any dramatic increase in support for the Left. Instead there was a redistribution of votes within the Left which pushed the radicals into third place with 1 422 000 votes, as against 1 502 000 for the communists and 1 964 000 for the socialists. Far from holding the reins of power, as they had expected, the radicals emerged as the great losers with 400 000 votes and 45 seats fewer than in 1932. With 106 deputies they were placed in a position where, at least initially, they could only participate in the coalition under Blum's leadership rather than lead it themselves.[24]

The Popular Front had always been both a mass movement and an electoral coalition, and the three Popular Front parties emerged from the elections with greatly differing ideas about the role of the Popular Front movement under a Popular Front government. The radicals felt that with the capture of government power the mass movement had served its purpose. The PCF by contrast, viewed things very differently. It was delighted with the results of an electoral coalition which had increased communist parliamentary representation sixfold, from 12 to 72 seats in the Chamber. But it also intended to continue with its effort to create a mass movement which would increase its influence and membership among the working class. In PCF eyes this was every bit as important as the winning of government power. Four months before the elections *L'Humanité* had explained how 'the Popular Front is the mobilisation of the masses . . . and not the ministerial participation which those organisations who claim to represent the working class are constantly offering us'.[25] When the offer of participation in government finally did come, the communists accordingly refused. Vaillant Couturier explained that, instead, the party would be 'alongside the government of the left, supporting it, assuring its stability, exercising from outside a sort of ministry of the masses'.[26] According to the communist historian, Serge Wolikow, the Comintern took the view that communist participation in a Popular Front government meant running the risk of 'destabilising it through arousing reactions from the Right [and] in tying the hands of the Party which in this situation would be incapable of being at one and the same time a governing party and a party of class struggle'.[27] The problem was that many of those middle-class people who had voted for the Popular Front felt that there was no room for a party of class struggle within the coalition regardless of whether it was inside or outside the cabinet.

Léon Blum was clear in his mind that the role of the Popular Front did not extend as far as class struggle. For Blum the Popular Front was a coalition with national aspirations which could not afford to represent the interests of any one party or class exclusively, and he saw his task as being strictly limited to the implementation of the Popular Front programme. In light of the fact that the socialists had been defeated over so many of their proposals for the programme, Blum's scrupulously loyal defence of it seemed surprising. Nevertheless, when he spoke to the SFIO conference which was held at the height of the May–June strike wave, Blum insisted that:

it is the Popular Front movement which has placed in Parliament the majority of which we will be the expression, and that the programme of the government will be precisely the common programme of the Popular Front . . . Our object, our mandate, our duty is to fulfil and carry out this programme.[28]

The theoretical basis of Blum's commitment to limit himself to implementing the Popular Front programme derived from his earlier reflections on the distinction between the 'conquest of power' which would accompany the revolution and the more immediately achievable aim of what he termed 'the exercise of power' within the established framework of French society. Blum was clear that the Popular Front only offered the opportunity for the exercise of power but he was acutely aware in 1936 of the problem that he had outlined ten years earlier when he had warned:

The danger of the exercise of power [is] precisely that it may be confused with the conquest of power, so that the proletariat is encouraged to expect from the former the totality of results which can result only from the latter.[29]

Blum's attitude towards the responsibilities of office was certainly intellectually consistent with the position he had held ten years earlier. But circumstances changed rapidly in 1936 and by the time he took office a strike movement was underway whose scope alone tended to call into question the previous distinctions between the conquest of power in a revolutionary situation and the mere exercise of power after an election. According to Blum's critics, the danger in May and June 1936 was less that the working class would mistake the exercise of power for its conquest than that Blum himself would be slow to exploit to the full the possibilities opened up for the 'exercise of power' at a time of unprecedented working-class mobilisation.[30]

THE POPULAR FRONT IN POWER

The Strikes of May and June 1936

The scale of the strikes was staggering. For the month of June alone 12 142 strikes were recorded involving 1.8 million workers.[31] In addition, over three quarters of the officially recorded strikes also involved the new and audacious tactic of factory occupations. Initially, occupations were restricted to large engineering factories but in time they extended to include cafés, department stores, and even ships in ports such as Marseilles were taken over by their crews who ran up the red flag on the mast.

The first occupation on 11 May at the Bréguet aircraft factory at Le Havre gave no hint of the scale of the movement that would develop, but it did provide evidence of a new mood among the working class. The Bréguet workers struck out of solidarity with fifteen of their colleagues who had been sacked for taking part in the May Day strike. Normally this kind of action by management would not have met with any reaction, especially in a factory like Bréguet where there was no history of militancy and where only fifteen out of the 600 workers had struck on May Day. But after the election of a Popular Front government, workers were more ready to defend their sacked colleagues and to challenge managerial authority.

The outcome of the strike also provided evidence of a changed situation. Within a day the local Mayor had arbitrated in favour of the workers, the sacked May Day strikers were reinstated and the occupation was concluded. Never before had a strike in Le Havre produced such a speedy victory for the workers. The benefits were also passed on to the local trade union which had helped in the organisation of the strike, since within a short time 90 per cent of Bréguet workers had joined the CGT.[32]

The action of the Bréguet workers was quickly copied by workers at other aircraft factories: first at Toulouse on 13 May and then at the Bloch factory at Courbevoie near Paris. After 28 May the strikes spread to the large car factories around Paris affecting Renault at Billancourt – France's largest factory – as well as Simca and Citroën. A settlement on 29 May produced only a temporary respite before the news of these successful early strikes helped to spread further strikes across the entire country. The sense of optimism and pent up frustration led to a constant escalation in workers' demands with some factories launching second strikes with new demands after their first strikes had been satisfactorily concluded. In other factories, workers went on strike before they had drawn up any demands at all, only doing so later in consultation with local trade unions and Popular Front committees. Demands varied greatly from factory to factory; they almost always included calls for wage rises and, often, for greater trade union rights, the independent assessment of time and motion studies, longer lunch breaks, shorter hours and paid holidays. Many strikers included the vague but revealing call simply for greater dignity – for employers and their foremen to show more respect towards the workers.

No one had anticipated a strike movement on such a scale and there is no evidence to suggest that it was part of a conspiracy organised by the PCF, the trade unions or the far Left aimed at seizing state power. Communist officials were themselves involved in attempts to bring the strikes to an early end, first in the agreement of 29 May and then again in the Matignon Agreement of 7 June. When the left socialist Marceau Pivert published his article on 27 May arguing that 'tout est possible', within 48 hours the PCF newspaper *L'Humanité* replied forcefully, 'Tout n'est pas possible', arguing that what was important was to implement the Popular Front programme rather than to act in a way which might provoke the collapse of the coalition even before it had entered government. In the last days of May, communist officials constantly warned of the dangers of disorder, of the need to bring the strikes to an early end and to avoid any action which might weaken France in the face of the threat posed by Nazi Germany.[33] When the strikes continued, even after the signing of the Matignon Agreement, Maurice Thorez called the movement to order, reminding communists that, 'il faut savoir terminer une grève', and travelling to various places such as Marseilles to try to achieve just that.[34]

While the strikes were not the result of a conspiracy, it would, however, be wrong to classify them as purely spontaneous. It is true that there was a notable lack of formal organisation and that the strikes were most intense in badly unionised industries such as engineering, textiles and food manufacturing, which had unionisation rates of 4, 5 and 3 per cent respectively.[35] But for years PCF and CGTU propaganda had been targeted precisely on these badly unionised sectors of manufacturing industry where the strikes began. These efforts had produced very little in the way of formal trade union or party membership but they did help to create a mood of militancy with an explosive potential. Communist activists at factories such as Renault in Paris, or the Coder engineering factory in Marseilles or in the mines of the Nord and Pas de Calais, saw May 1936 as the opportunity they had been waiting for to increase their influence among the working class by the organisation of successful strikes.[36] Of course, many strikes occurred in factories where there were no politically active workers; but, equally, when there were communist activists they tended to work hard to increase the militancy of the workforce and played a key role in the organisation of the strikes. Once strikes had been started party policy dictated that PCF members should be equally active in trying to bring them to an early end. Party members often found it difficult to resolve these two roles, and some of them, disappointed that the party had not attempted revolution, decided to leave the PCF. But for the most part, the PCF emerged at the end of June in a satisfactory position, with its membership and influence among the working class greatly enhanced by its role during the strikes.[37]

Whereas the communists could be active both in the strike movement and in trying to bring it to an early end, the socialists, as a party of government as well as of the working class, had to behave in a rather more straightforward way. A few days before he took office, the SFIO Minister of the Interior, Roger Salengro, set the tone when he expressed his hope:

That those whose task it is to lead the working class will do their duty. That they will make haste to bring this unjustified agitation to an end . . . For my part I've made my choice between order and anarchy. I will maintain order in the face of all opposition.[38]

In reality, as Blum discovered when he took office, there were just not enough troops to restore order by force.[39] The only hope of ending the strikes lay in a national agreement negotiated between the CGT and the employers.

It was the employers' representatives who requested the meeting with the CGT which took place on 7 June at the Prime Minister's office in the Hôtel Matignon. The 'agreement' which emerged was a barely veiled climbdown by the employers before the demands both of government and unions. The latter agreed that they would respect the law in return for a commitment by the employers to honour trade union rights. There was also provision for the negotiation of collective agreements by region and by industry, for an increase in wages ranging from 15 per cent for the lowest paid workers to 7 per cent for the highest paid, and for a system of works delegates to be elected by all workers in factories employing more than ten people. The CGT called on workers to end their strikes as soon as the national agreement could be applied locally, while Blum promised the CGT that the government would immediately introduce laws to regulate the new collective contracts and to enact the forty-hour week and paid holidays.[40]

The Matignon Agreement did not produce an immediate end to the factory occupations but it did signal a dramatic change in the balance of political and industrial power. The most obvious change was simply the fact that the CGT had met with employers' representatives in the presence of an openly sympathetic government and without its own claims to represent workers being called into question. The system of collective contracts effectively recognised the CGT as the most representative union and gave it the power to negotiate agreements which could be applied to entire industries or regions. The system of works delegates, or shop stewards, also tended to increase the CGT's authority. These and other measures all helped to consolidate and extend the astonishing growth in the CGT's membership. At Renault's Billancourt factory, for example, while only 700 of the 33 000 workers were members of the CGT before the strikes, the figure afterwards was near to 25 000, increasing again to 31 000 by the end of the year. Nationally, the CGT increased its membership from around 750 000 at the beginning of 1936 to almost 4 000 000 a year later.[41]

While Matignon attests to the way in which the strikes had tilted the balance of industrial power in favour of the working class and its organisations, this was not a change which employers were ready to accept. Many saw the June strikes as a near revolutionary movement which had flouted their authority and violated their property rights, and they reproached their representatives at Matignon for having given away too much, too easily. This criticism set the tone for the following months. Most employers emerged from the strikes feeling humiliated, bitter and betrayed. Their attitudes thereafter would be more often motivated by hatred than by a desire for harmony.[42]

The feelings of employers were, of course, reflected in the community at large as well as in the political arena. For the middle class, the combination of the election of the Popular Front government and the strike wave which followed it produced a sense of hysteria and collective fear of a kind not seen since the Commune of 1871.[43] In the National Assembly the same reaction of fear led to the rapid acceptance of the provisions of the Matignon Agreement and of almost the entire Popular Front programme. In addition, measures which had been opposed for years and which did not even feature in the programme, such as the laws on paid holidays and collective contracts, were passed with minimal opposition and in record time.[44] Interestingly, Blum's honeymoon with the National Assembly ended over the vote for a National Wheat Office – a measure which had featured in the programme but which the Senate had resisted from late July until mid-August. The delay revealed the way in which the ending of the factory occupations had restored the opposition's self-confidence and replaced the unanimity born of fear evident in June 1936 with the spirit of resistance – and even retribution.

Léon Blum was slow to realise the extent to which the strikes of June 1936 had polarised French politics. He assumed that by remaining scrupulously faithful to the requirements both of bourgeois legality and of the Popular Front programme he might succeed in winning the cooperation of employers and financiers, thereby holding the Popular Front coalition together.[45] But these aspirations, the products of Blum's

legal training, and his reflections on the 'exercise of power', were
overtaken by events almost as soon as he entered government. The
strikers had flouted established legality and won. The Popular Front
programme had not only been passed in record time, it had been
exceeded into the bargain.

In this situation Blum's earlier reflections on the 'exercise of power'
seemed to blind him to the political realities around him. The opposition
and the employers were looking for revenge rather than reconciliation.
The middle class radicals who had been painstakingly won over to the
Popular Front were uneasy. And the working class, having rediscovered
its power and self-confidence, seemed reluctant to embrace a legality
which might deny it access to the tools of direct action which had proved
so fruitful during May and June.

The Spanish Crisis

The outbreak of the Spanish Civil War just six weeks after Blum took
office tended to increase still further the atmosphere of political
polarisation and class conflict created by the strikes. While the latter had
posed in acute form the unresolved question of class relations within the
Popular Front, the Spanish crisis tested it at its ideological weak point –
on the issue of anti-fascism.

Blum's initial response to Franco's uprising was to help the Popular
Front government in Spain by honouring an order for the delivery of 20
million francs worth of military aircraft and other munitions. The
decision seemed to accord both with France's right under international
law to provide help for the legitimately elected government of Spain and
with Blum's own desire to help the Spanish Republic defend itself
against fascism. But after the government's intentions had been leaked
to the right-wing press, the pressure on Blum to abandon the Republic
increased. The British made known their hostility to any French
government help, while the Quai D'Orsay warned of the danger that
Germany and Italy might be prompted to help Franco if France
delivered planes to the Republic. Within his own cabinet, Blum had to
face the opposition of many of his Radical Party ministers. One of them,
Camille Chautemps, put it to Blum that, 'No one will understand . . . if
we go and run the risk of war for Spain when we did not over the
[remilitarisation of the] Rhineland'.[46] Faced with this opposition Blum
revised his policy and suspended the delivery of military aid to Spain.
When evidence emerged in August that Italy was in fact giving military
support to Franco, Blum's response was to try to organise an agreement

on non-intervention that would involve all the major European powers. By early September a total of 24 nations including Germany, Italy, Britain and the Soviet Union had put their names to the French initiative on non-intervention.[47]

The decision not to intervene in the Spanish conflict was one of the most difficult of Blum's career and it drove him to the verge of resigning. His natural inclination was to help the sister Popular Front government in Spain in its struggle against fascism. But he felt that to provide such help would bring the danger of a European war that much closer, and also weaken France's position internationally by dividing it from its ally in Britain. Domestically Blum feared that intervention would provoke the collapse of the government and even produce a civil war in France itself.

Within France the non-intervention policy was attacked by many of the government's supporters as a betrayal of the anti-fascist principles on which the Popular Front had been founded. The criticism intensified at the beginning of September, as the news of the fall of Irún, just across the border from France, brought home the seriousness of the crisis. The communists led the way in attacking the policy of non-intervention, producing thousands of leaflets and posters calling for weapons for Spain and holding repeated demonstrations in support of the Spanish Republic. Blum experienced the campaign at first hand when he attended a socialist rally at Luna Park on 6 September, the day after the fall of Irún. The audience included the left-wing socialists of the Seine Federation of the SFIO, as well as a good number of communists. Blum's arrival was greeted by cries of 'Blum à l'action' and 'Des avions pour l'Espagne'.[48] When Blum took the platform he delivered an anguished speech in which he argued that non-intervention, rather than a mad rush to supply the combatants, was the best guarantee that the legal government would triumph and that intervention would only aggravate the international situation. He took issue with those belligerent anti-fascists who suggested that France should stand up against the dictatorship instead of constantly making concessions by reminding his audience that it was not for nothing that socialists had campaigned for fifteen years for peace through negotiation rather than through military efforts. But Blum also complemented this assertion of socialist pacifist anti-fascism with the, by now familiar, reminder of the limitations of his office, and the fact that as Prime Minister he had obligations to the nation as well as to the party.[49]

Within just a few weeks it became clear that non-intervention was ineffective. By the end of September there was ample evidence of

Mussolini's many violations of the non-intervention agreement and the Soviet Union, for its part, had decided to supply the Spanish Republic with weapons. Blum too, while continuing to support the principle of non-intervention, in fact gave secret instructions to French customs officers to allow material to cross the border into Spain. For Blum this gesture made the official policy more bearable but it also undermined French claims to neutrality and weakened the absoluteness of their case against Axis intervention in Spain.[50]

While non-intervention was not a morally attractive policy, nor even a very effective one, it probably did reflect the strong desire for peace which was felt by the French population.[51] But the government's reaction to the Spanish crisis also blunted the all-conquering optimism and the spirit of unity which the election victory and the strikes had produced among the Popular Front's working-class supporters. Disagreements over policy towards Spain helped to provoke the re-emergence of divisions within the trade unions between the communist advocates of aid for Spain and those elements of the SFIO and the CGT who were opposed to anything they thought might turn into an anti-fascist crusade which would conflict with their entrenched pacifism. In October the anti-communist and pacifist elements, under the leadership of René Belin of the CGT Secretariat, started their own factional trade union newspaper, *Syndicats*, which aimed to counter the growing influence of the communist trade union newspaper, *La Vie Ouvrière*.[52] In the parliamentary arena, meanwhile, Spain caused the first major open division within the Popular Front when, on 5 December, the communist deputies abstained in a vote over the government's Spanish policy. This clear division over policy towards Spain highlighted the fact that the Popular Front's attempts to ally the principles of anti-fascism and pacifism had been no more successful in providing the basis for a long-lasting government than its belief in the need for a cross-class alliance had been.

SEPTEMBER TO THE FALL OF BLUM

The last nine months of Blum's government, from September 1936 to June 1937, saw him trimming policy in the domestic arena to meet the criticisms of his Radical Party colleagues and the opposition, in the same way that he had done in the area of foreign policy over Spain. The motivation for Blum's moderation was his desire for a greater degree of national unity and reconciliation. But the political results of his strategy were disappointing. Blum's opponents simply read his moderation as a sign of weakness and they were encouraged to go on to the offensive. Meanwhile, many of his working-class supporters interpreted moderation as akin to betrayal and their willingness to support the government declined accordingly.

September provided few signs of the kind of reconciliation that Blum had sought. While the Prime Minister and his colleagues had spent August dealing with the Spanish crisis, the employers had been planning their revenge for the humiliation they had suffered during June. Their anger was reflected within their own organisation, the CGPF, which was recast and renamed, while its President, René Duchemin, who had represented the employers in the Matignon negotiations, was sacked and replaced by the more abrasive Claude Gignoux. This new mood was also reflected in individual factories where many employers spent the autumn trying to claw back the concessions granted in June.[53]

The new employer militancy, together with the effects of inflation (retail prices increased by 5.5 per cent from May to September) and the PCF campaign against non-intervention in Spain, combined to spark off a new wave of strikes in September.[54] Once again the strikes started in the engineering industry but they lacked the unanimity and jubilation of June. This time many of the strikes tended to be tightly organised by the PCF and conducted in the face of opposition from employers, the CGT, the government and, indeed, from many of the workers themselves.[55]

This revival of industrial conflict worried both the government and the CGT. The government was concerned about the damage that the strikes would do to its efforts to promote economic recovery and national reconciliation. The CGT, for its part, was disturbed by signs that the PCF might use its influence in the factories to outflank the official trade union movement and embarrass the government.[56]

Moves during the autumn to institute a system of compulsory arbitration in labour disputes were designed to resolve at least some of these problems. Traditionally the CGT had been opposed to compulsory arbitration – seeing it as a feature of fascist regimes where unions had no existence independent of the state. But after the experience of June, when the new Popular Front government and its officials had frequently intervened on behalf of labour, the CGT leadership came to believe that arbitration could offer a way of satisfying workers' grievances without risking protracted and politically damaging strikes. In union eyes there seemed no question but that compulsory arbitration would tend to favour workers against employers.[57]

In practice, however, the arbitration system operated in a far less favourable way than the unions had anticipated. Joel Colton has described how: 'The expectation that arbitrators under a Popular Front sponsored arbitration system might throw caution to the winds and serve only the interests of the labour movement proved to be unfounded. The very opposite proved to be the case.' The results were particularly noticeable in the area of wage demands. Colton found that where any increases were granted they were on average only a half to two thirds of that registered by the cost of living index. In his view, 'There is no doubt that the excessive caution of the arbitrators and a consuming concern for preventing inflation resulted in many instances in injustice to labour.'[58]

The injustices of the arbitration system obviously proved a great disappointment to workers and trade unions alike and in time they contributed to the erosion of confidence in the Blum government. But the whole operation of the system also pointed up a cruel irony: at the very moment when labour had finally reconciled itself with the state, the government was in the process of embracing a notion of the national interest which placed great emphasis on the need for increasing production and profitability and left little room for meeting the demands of the working class. The new mood of the government was hinted at by Blum in a speech he made to a Radical Party meeting in October, where he said that after 'the immense changes which we have introduced into economic and social life, the prosperity of the country, the health of the country, now demands a sufficient period of stability, of normality'.[59]

Blum's desire to slow down the pace of reform derived in part from his belief in the limitations of the exercise of power, but it was also prompted by his concern to restore financial confidence. The decision of June 1936 to remain loyal to the Popular Front programme by not introducing coercive financial measures – such as exchange controls – had left the currency vulnerable to speculation. The combination of the June strikes and the Spanish crisis prompted a flight of capital which reduced the Bank of France's gold reserves from almost 63 billion francs in April to around 54 billion at the beginning of September. When a further 1.5 billion left the country from 4 to 16 September, Blum was forced to do what he had promised he never would: devalue the franc by between 25 and 35 per cent.[60] The devaluation antagonised everyone. The Right said it was his punishment for financial profligacy while many socialists and communists were hostile to a measure which they believed would increase prices and hit the pockets of the poor.[61]

Blum was most concerned by the way in which the devaluation increased support for those elements within the Radical Party who had always been hostile to the Popular Front. They re-emerged into the open during the last week of October at the party's Biarritz conference, where they called for a change in policy and insisted that the interests of small businessmen, peasants and retired people should not be sacrificed for the sake of improvements in working-class living standards. There were more strident calls too, with claims that the party had been duped into taking part in a Popular Front dominated by the communists designed to create a Soviet-style society.[62] In the end, Daladier and those Radicals who were favourable to the Popular Front carried the day but the closing resolution of the conference made it clear that this support was conditional on a change in the political situation, an end to strikes and occupations, a cessation of communist attacks on the policy of non-intervention, and a promise by the government to pay more attention to the needs of the middle classes.[63]

Blum chose to heed Radical calls for moderation rather than the calls of those within his own party, like Marceau Pivert, who were warning that he had to choose between 'taking the offensive or capitulating'.[64] His New Year message for 1937 marked a firm rejection of left-wing calls for further reforms. Instead he sought reconciliation, presenting his reforms as nothing more than an advanced form of economic liberalism carried out by what he described as a truly national government.[65] Blum's 'national' aspirations were reflected in his call in February for a 'pause' in reforms so that private industry could recover from the dual shock of the Matignon reforms and the devaluation, and so that the government could organise rearmament.[66]

In practice, the financial measures announced in March revealed the pause to be a return to traditional rather than 'advanced' economic liberalism. The government promised to balance the budget by cutting back on expenditure. A special loan was mounted, free trade in gold was re-established, and three conservative financial experts were put in charge of overseeing currency dealings at the Bank of France. In addition, measures which had been included in the Popular Front programme to improve or provide pensions, unemployment benefit, the indexation of wages, and a programme of public works, were all either cancelled or cut back. The newspaper, *Le Temps*, commented, 'It's more than a pause, it's a conversion!'[67]

Conversion or not, the 'pause' was a clear offer of reconciliation to the middle class and the employers. But within a few days of the announcement of the March financial measures, riots at Clichy undermined the chances for a restoration of either middle-class or working-class confidence in the government. The incidents developed on the evening of 16 May when communists and socialists demonstrated in Clichy against the holding of a Parti Social Français meeting (formerly the Croix de Feu) which local councillors had unsuccessfully attempted to have banned. Violence broke out when some of the demonstrators tried to break up the meeting, the police intervened and shots were fired which resulted in five deaths and two hundred injuries. It it still unclear who was responsible for the violence, but the riots left the government even more isolated as the Left blamed it for having used the police against the demonstrators while the Right and the Radical Party accused the government of being incapable of preventing its supporters from rioting. The effect of the riots was clearest on the financial markets. The Bourse registered a sharp drop, more capital fled the country and investors were reluctant to subscribe to the new government loan.[68]

Clichy killed off any chance of a revival of confidence among the middle classes. It also fuelled the mounting hostility to Blum within the Radical Party. A meeting called by the Young Radical Socialists at Carcassonne in April had been attended by no less than thirty Radical Party members of the National Assembly who were keen to 'restore the party's autonomy' by breaking with the Popular Front.[69] As the increasing disgruntlement of the rank-and-file made itself felt, deputies who had previously been committed to the Popular Front started stepping up their attacks on the socialists. On 6 June the party's President, Daladier, joined in the criticism when he spoke at Saint Gaudens at a meeting called by the party's south-western federation which was well known for its hostility to the Popular Front. Although, as Deputy Prime Minister, Daladier was careful to avoid a direct attack on the government, his comments about the need to restore order and about the failure of the French economy to share in the recovery her neighbours were experiencing, were widely interpreted as an indication that he would no longer stand in the way of attempts to bring down the government.[70]

Blum's opponents finally triumphed on 22 June when Radical Party defections in the Senate led the Upper House to refuse him the decree powers, already approved by the Chamber, to deal with the financial panic. But if the Radical Senators felt able to oppose Blum in June 1937 when they had not done so before, it is fair to assume that their decision was made in the knowledge that it reflected the wishes both of the party's rank-and-file and of its deputies in the Chamber. While Blum was voted down by the Senate there was a sense in which this merely reflected the shift of opinion within the Radical Party as a whole, since it was easier for indirectly elected Senators to oppose Blum openly than it was for their colleagues in the Chamber – many of whom owed their seats to Popular Front electoral alliances at the local level. When Blum asked his Radical cabinet colleagues whether he should resist the Senate, in the first instance by calling for another vote of confidence in the Chamber and then, if necessary, by dissolving and calling fresh elections, their decision to resign made it clear that they too shared the Senate's hostile view. Faced with this collapse in his majority Blum resigned, to be replaced immediately by his former Minister of State, the Radical Camille Chautemps. Significantly, Chautemps was granted almost immediately the decree powers which enabled him to carry out the devaluation that Blum had been denied.[71]

CONCLUSION

Blum's fall from office effectively marked the end of the Popular Front, but it also helped to dispel some of his own misconceptions, both about the nature of the Popular Front itself, and about French politics in the 1930s, which had themselves contributed to the failure of his government.

Unlike his coalition partners, Blum had taken seriously the rallying cries for the union of the entire French people against the two hundred families, against fascism, and in defence of the Republic, believing that the ideals of national unity and consensus which underlay these slogans were indeed attainable if he remained scrupulously faithful to the Popular Front programme. Blum's approach fitted in well with his previous decade of reflection on the limitations involved in the 'exercise of power', but it ignored both the political realities of the time and indeed the political dynamic created by the Popular Front itself. Even before Blum took office the Popular Front was flawed by the fact that the parties which composed it had very different positions *vis-à-vis* the fundamental issues of anti-fascism, republicanism and class interest on which it was based. Even more seriously, the parties disagreed over the status of the Popular Front programme. For the communists it was simply a tactical measure to reassure the Radicals. Radical Party politicians viewed it as neither 'an electoral programme, nor a governmental programme, nor indeed a programme at all'.[72] Blum, for his part, made the programme the final arbiter of his actions, keeping it on his desk when Prime Minister, referring to it whenever a proposal was put to him, always asking, 'Is it or is it not in the programme?'[73]

Given the precarious nature of the Popular Front, Blum's legalistic attachment to its programme appears naive, and after the June strikes, this naivety was also politically damaging. The strikes polarised opinions and antagonised the middle class and employers to such an extent that Blum's quest for consensus became meaningless. Indeed, while the initial fear generated by the strikes had helped to win rapid acceptance for the reforms, Blum's failure to exploit this to the full, and his moderation thereafter, served simply to fuel the hostility of his opponents rather than winning their confidence as he had hoped. Meanwhile his working-class supporters became increasingly disillusioned: over Spain, over the arbitration system, and because of the slowing down in the pace of reform. The atmosphere when Blum resigned was very different from that of the previous summer. In June 1937 there were no demonstrations in support of Blum and no strikes in protest at his dismissal by the Senate. Blum's loyalty to the Popular Front programme had won him neither the approval of his supporters nor the acceptance he sought from his opponents. In his wartime writings Blum reflected on the political reality that he had refused to come to terms with in 1936, namely that in interwar France it was the bourgeoisie which held power and it was unwilling to relinquish or even to share it. In such a situation the 'exercise of power' seemed to make little sense. As Blum himself put it, even when the Left won a majority in the Chamber, 'the bourgeoisie retained the means of resistance which only temporarily gave way to fear, and which recovered their effectiveness as soon as the fear subsided'.[74]

Notes

1. P. Warwick, *The French Popular Front: A Legislative Analysis* (Chicago, 1977) p. 24.
2. H. Dubief, *Le déclin de la IIIe Republique, 1929–1938* (Paris, 1976) pp. 76–7.
3. *Le Populaire*, 11 February 1934.
4. *L'Humanité*, 1 March 1934 boasted of how 700 workers had joined the PCF in the aftermath of the 12 February demonstration and strike.
5. *L'Humanité*, 6 February 1934 cited by N. Racine and L. Bodin, *Le Parti Communiste Français pendant l'entre-deux-guerres* (Paris, 1972) p. 206.
6. *L'Humanité*, 19 February 1934, cited in ibid.
7. The very term 'Popular Front' was supplied by the Comintern liaison officer in France, Eugen Fried.
8. Léon Blum experienced what he described as 'a complicated mixture of hope

and anxiety' faced with a change for which he could find no 'absolutely satisfactory explanation'. *Le Populaire*, 20 July 1934, cited by J. Joll, *Three Intellectuals in Politics* (New York, 1960) pp. 32–3.

9. Jacques Doriot was expelled from the party at the June Conference, see J.-P. Brunet, 'Réflexions sur la scission de Doriot', *Le Mouvement social* (1970) pp. 62–3. For examples of the PCF's attacks on the SFIO see, P. Robrieux, *Maurice Thorez, Vie secrète et vie publique* (Paris, 1975) pp. 188–9.

10. P. Robrieux, *Histoire intérieure du parti communiste, tome 1, 1920–1945* (Paris, 1980) pp. 456–7.

11. Cited by J. Joll, 'The Front Populaire – After Thirty Years', *Journal of Contemporary History* (1966) p. 27.

12. S. Berstein, *Histoire du Parti Radical*, tome 2 (Paris, 1982) p. 373.

13. The communiqué proposed by Laval and accepted by Stalin stated that: 'Stalin understands and approves fully the policy of national defence undertaken by France to maintain armed forces adequate for her security'. Cited by M. Baumont, *The Origins of the Second World War* (New Haven, 1978) p. 131.

14. *Le Populaire*, 17 May 1935, cited by N. Greene, *Crisis and Decline: The French Socialist Party in the Popular Front Era* (Ithaca, 1969) p. 27.

15. For a critical assessment of Léon Blum's own attitude towards Hitler's rise to power see, J. Bariety, 'Léon Blum et l'Allemagne, 1930–1938', in *Les Relations Franco–Allemandes, 1933–1939* (Paris, 1976) pp. 33–55.

16. Pierre Boivin, cited by Jacques Droz, *Histoire de l'antifascisme en Europe, 1923–1939* (Paris, 1985) p. 195.

17. R. Gombin, *Les Socialistes et la Guerre* (Paris, 1970) p. 211.

18. P. Birnbaum, *Le Peuple et Les Gros: Histoire d'un mythe* (Paris, 1979) pp. 27, 35.

19. Ibid., p. 29.

20. *Le Populaire*, 5 April 1936, cited by Birnbaum, *Le Peuple et Les Gros*, p. 47.

21. Berstein, *Histoire du Parti Radical*, p. 389. Maurice Thorez boasted of the PCF's moderation, saying 'that the Communists were seen refusing to write into the programme of the Popular Front the socializations which certain people urged', cited by D. Brower, *The New Jacobins: The French Communist Party and the Popular Front* (Ithaca, 1968) p. 117.

22. The programme is printed in full in the best general history of the period, G. Lefranc, *Histoire du Front Populaire, (1934–1938)* (Paris, 1974) pp. 475–9.

23. Berstein, *Histoire du Parti Radical*, pp. 427, 433–5.

24. Ibid., pp. 436–44.

25. *L'Humanité*, 4–5 January 1936.

26. *L'Humanité*, 17 May 1936, cited by Racine and Bodin, *Le Parti Communiste Français*, p. 210.

27. S. Wolikow, 'Le P.C.F. et le Front populaire', in R. Bourderon *et al.*, *Le P.C.F. étapes et problèmes, 1920–1972* (Paris, 1981) p. 175.

28. *Oeuvre de Léon Blum, tome 4i*, Speech, 31 May 1936, pp. 260–1.

29. Cited by Joll, 'The Front Populaire', p. 35. On the 'exercise of power' see also G. Ziebura, *Léon Blum et le Parti Socialiste, 1872–1934* (Paris, 1967) p. 286.

30. Compare the comments of Marceau Pivert at the SFIO Congress held from 30 May to 1 June 1936: 'Nous allons exercer le pouvoir dans le régime

bourgeois mais . . . cet exercice du pouvoir ne vaudrait rien, il n'aurait aucun intérêt pour le Parti socialiste s'il ne constituait pas un élément de la marche directe à la conquête du pouvoir.' Cited by G. Dupeux, 'Léon Blum et la majorité parlementaire', in *Colloque, Léon Blum: Chef de Gouvernement, 1936–1937* (Paris, 1967) p. 111.

31. In reality the figure was probably higher since the Préfectures were so overwhelmed with work in June 1936 that their statistics were rather incomplete.

32. F. Cahier, 'La classe ouvrière Havraise et le Front Populaire, 1934–1938', *Mémoire de maîtrise* (Université de Paris, I, 1972) pp. 43–7.

33. J. Fauvet, *Histoire du parti communiste français, tome I* (Paris, 1964) pp. 198–9.

34. D. A. L. Levy, 'The Marseilles Working Class Movement, 1936–1938', DPhil. thesis, Oxford University, 1983, p. 269.

35. Industries such as the railways, post office and public utilities, with unionisation rates of 22, 44, and 36 per cent respectively, did not strike at all. See A. Prost, 'Les grèves de juin 1936, essai d'interprétation', in *Colloque, Léon Blum*, p. 73.

36. See the following sources concerning communist influence in the strikes. B. Badie, 'Les grèves du Front Populaire aux usines Renault', *Le mouvement social* (1972) pp. 69–109; R. Hainsworth, 'Les grèves du Front Populaire de mai et juin 1936', *Le mouvement social* (1976) pp. 3–30, and D. A. L. Levy, 'The Marseilles Working Class Movement', pp. 213–70.

37. The PCF increased its membership from around 90 000 in February to 250 000 in September 1936. A Kriegel, 'Le parti communiste sous la *IIIe* Republique (1920–1939): Mouvement des effectifs et structures d'organisation', in A. Kriegel, *Le pain et les roses: Jalons pour une histoire des socialismes* (Paris, 1972) pp. 311–14.

38. Cited by Lefranc, *Histoire du Front Populaire*, p. 146.

39. See the comments of Gaston Cusin in *Colloque, Léon Blum*, p. 293.

40. René Belin gives a good first-hand account of the Matignon negotiations in his book, *Du secretariat de la CGT au Gouvernement de Vichy* (Paris, 1978) pp. 97–103.

41. Renault figures from Badie, 'Les grèves du Front Populaire'; National CGT figures in A. Prost, *La CGT a l'époque du Front Populaire* (Paris, 1964).

42. See the comments of Pierre Waline in *Colloque, Léon Blum*, p. 284. Also Waline's comments at the time, reprinted in the same source pp. 316–17.

43. L. Bodin and J. Touchard, 'L'état de l'opinion au debut de l'année 1936', in *Colloque, Léon Blum*, pp. 61–2.

44. E. Gout *et al.*, 'La politique sociale du Front Populaire', in *Colloque, Léon Blum*, pp. 247–9.

45. G. Dupeux, 'L'échec du premier Gouvernement Léon Blum', *Revue d'Histoire Moderne et Contemporaine* (1963) p. 40.

46. Cited by D. W. Pike, *Les français et la guerre d'Espagne, 1936–1939* (Paris, 1975) p. 372.

47. J.-B. Duroselle, *Politique estrangère de la France: La décadence, 1932–1939* (Paris, 1983) p. 303.

48. J. Lacouture, *Léon Blum* (Paris, 1984) pp. 362–3.

49. Ibid., p. 364.

50. Pike, *Les français et la guerre d'Espagne*, p. 369.

51. Ibid., pp. 373–4.

52. M-F. Rogliano, 'L'anticommunisme dans la CGT: Syndicats', *Le mouvement social* (1974) pp. 63–84.

53. B. Brizay, *Le patronat* (Paris, 1975) pp. 46–9.

54. J.-B. Duroselle, *Politique etrangère*, p. 305; J. Colton, *Compulsory Labor Arbitration in France, 1936–1939* (New York, 1951) p. 33.

55. D. A. L. Levy, 'The Marseilles Working Class Movement', pp. 271–8. Lefranc, *Histoire du Front Populaire*, p. 199.

56. B. Georges *et al.*, *Léon Jouhaux dans le mouvement syndical Français* (Paris, 1979) pp. 174–6.

57. Colton, *Compulsory Labor Arbitration*, p. 37.

58. Ibid., p. 86.

59. Cited by Lefranc, *Histoire du Front Populaire*, p. 207.

60. Dubief, *Le declin de la IIIe Republique*, p. 200.

61. Lefranc. *Histoire du Front Populaire*, p. 201.

62. Berstein, *Histoire du Parti Radical*, pp. 462–3, 480.

63. Ibid., p. 484.

64. See Thorez's speech of 27 January 1937, cited by Lefranc, *Histoire du Front Populaire*, p. 226; and *Le Populaire*, 25 December 1936, cited by Dupeux in *Colloque, Léon Blum*, p. 117.

65. See Dupeux, 'L'échec du premier Gouvernement Léon Blum', p. 41.

66. Lefranc, *Histoire du Front Populaire*, pp. 228–30.

67. Cited by Dubief. *Le declin de la IIIe Republique*, p. 202

68. Brower, *The New Jacobins*, pp. 182–4.

69. Berstein, *Histoire du Parti Radical*, pp. 496–7.

70. Ibid., pp. 499–500.

71. Dubief, *Le declin de la IIIe Republique*, pp. 208–11, Berstein, *Histoire du Parti Radical*, pp. 500–3.

72. Ibid., p. 388.

73. André Blumel, in *Colloque, Léon Blum*, p. 161.

74. Quoted by Dupeux, 'L'échec du premier Gouvernement Léon Blum', pp. 42–3.

5 The Creation of the Popular Front in Spain

Paul Preston

The adoption of the Popular Front strategy at the Seventh Congress of the Comintern in July and August 1935 ensured that popular frontism would be thereafter inevitably and inextricably associated with the international communist movement. Of the two countries where the strategy had greatest success, the more dramatic and long-lived experiment was indisputably that of Spain. In consequence, the war against the Spanish Popular Front, launched in 1936 by a right wing infuriated that it could not defend its material interests by legal electoral means, was widely assumed at the time and since to be a war against communism. It is true that the abandonment of the Spanish Republic by the Western democracies threw it into the arms of the Soviet Union and thus gave substance to the association of the republican cause with communism. However, at the time of the formation of what came to be known only belatedly as the Popular Front, the Communist Party played merely a peripheral role. It served the purposes of anti-republicans, and of the communists themselves, to argue otherwise. None the less, the truth is that the victorious left-wing electoral coalition of February 1936 was a revival of an earlier Republican–Socialist alliance and its formation was well under way when popular frontism was invented. It was the work, not of the communists, but of the moderate socialist Indalecio Prieto and, above all, of the republican ex-Prime Minister Manuel Azaña, both of whom wished to keep communist participation to the barest minimum simply because it could bring few votes to the coalition and would frighten many potential supporters.[1]

Nothing more clearly underlines this nor more directly indicates the importance of the service rendered to the Second Spanish Republic by Manuel Azaña than the hatred directed against him by the ideologues and publicists of the Francoist cause. The venomous slanders to which he was subjected during the civil war and long after his death are evidence that the enemies of the Republic recognised in him one of its greatest bulwarks. Azaña's most crucial contribution to the Second Republic was the inspiration and energy which he brought to the left-wing electoral coalition of 1936, the so-called Popular Front. The psychotically hostile description of Azaña made by the Francoist propagandist Joaquín Arrarás is extremely revealing in this respect:

> bastard foetus elevated to the highest office of an abject Republic by a corrupted and corrupting pseudodemocratic suffrage. Let us say to be exact that Azaña was the abortion of masonic lodges and the Internationals, the genuine president of the Republic of the Popular Front, the repulsive caterpillar of the red Spain of murders and secret police, of refined satanic cruelties.[2]

Another Francoist, in discussing the close identification of Azaña and the Republic, referred to him as 'a monster . . . who sums up, concentrates and symbolises all the guilt and all the sins . . . who gave tone and sense, shape and essence to the Spanish Republic', and attributed to him the credit for inspiring the Popular Front 'in the filthy waters of his sewer', 'preparing his pieces and moving his pawns'.[3] The divisions of the Left in the elections of November 1933 had ensured the victory of the authoritarian Catholic CEDA (Confederación Española de Derechas Autónomas) and of the corrupt Radical Party. Throughout 1934 and 1935, the Radical–CEDA coalition attempted the legal introduction of a reactionary corporative state.[4] The creation of the Popular Front, and the subsequent electoral victory of February 1936, prevented the completion of that process. It is hardly surprising then that Azaña should have been the target of such intense right-wing hatred.

The attribution of Azaña's great achievement to the communists is somewhat more puzzling. The Francoist view of the Popular Front is symbolised by the celebrated portrayal of it by the nationalist artist Carlos Saenz de Tejada as a death-bearing cavalry of Mongol hordes in Red Army uniform waving communist banners.[5] For Joaquín Arrarás, the Popular Front was nothing but 'the creation of the Communist International'.[6] Perhaps the Francoists' hatred of communism surpassed their phobia of Azaña, or perhaps they thought to express their enmity more virulently by associating him with what they chose to describe as a communist plot. Whatever the case, the communist movement was only too happy to attribute to itself the credit for the creation of the Spanish Popular Front.[7] Since the PCE (Partido Comunista de España) was, between 1935 and the beginning of 1936, an extremely small entity somewhat on the margins of the Spanish workers' movement, it is understandable that official party statements should try to capture the role of creating the Popular Front.

The readiness of the communists to take a credit which properly belongs to Azaña is – like the hatred of the Francoists – a tribute to the importance of the man's work in forging left-wing unity during 1935. Beyond the exaggerations of both Francoist and communist historiography, the contribution of Azaña to the creation of the Popular Front was acknowledged some time ago.[8] It is the purpose of this chapter to stress even further the importance of his efforts, together with those of the moderate socialist Indalecio Prieto, to save the Second Republic from slow conversion into a state resembling Dollfuss's Austria, by the creation of an electoral alliance capable of mobilising the great popular desire evident throughout 1935 for the recuperation of the Republic of 1931–33.

Prieto made considerable sacrifices to maintain the existing electoral coalition with the republican forces, despite his awareness of the limited commitment of many republicans to fundamental change in Spain. Prieto's labours were a continuation of his earlier collaboration with republican forces against the dictatorship of General Primo de Rivera and of his part in the creation of the Republican–Socialist Pact of San Sebastián in 1930 which effectively ensured a transition from the monarchy in 1931. They were the logical sequel to his efforts to prevent a breakdown of the Republican–Socialist understanding before the elections of November 1933. However, the construction of the Popular Front was a more difficult task than the others, because it had to be done against the opposition of the militant sections of the socialist movement, led by Francisco Largo Caballero.

The polemic between 'reformist' collaboration with the republicans and 'revolutionary' abstentionism or isolationism had a long history in the Spanish socialist movement. Before 1931, however, the issues at stake were less dramatic than during the Republic. Ultimately, it was a question of different tactical approaches to the problem of how a minority socialist movement could make its voice heard in a reactionary constitutional regime dominated by the monarchist parties who maintained their hegemony through the twin weapons of electoral falsification and repression. After 1931, however, the polemic came to assume the proportions of a life-or-death struggle which hinged on the broader issues of the nature of republicanism and the Republic. There were three main segments of the socialist movement. The right wing, with some strength in traditional craft unions, particularly the printers, sheltered behind the rigidly Marxist–Kautskyist analyses of the university philosopher, Julián Besteiro. The pragmatic centre, with substantial support among Asturian coalminers and Basque steelworkers, was led by Prieto and Fernando de los Ríos who had a considerable power base in Granada. The left wing consisted of the PSOE's radical youth movement – the Federación de Juventudes Socialistas, the Madrid PSOE group – the Agrupación Socialista Madrileña – and controlled numerous powerful unions, agricultural day labourers, construction workers and metalworkers among others, all under the leadership of Francisco Largo Caballero, whose narrowly syndicalist/workerist options led to his being on the far left in 1934, just as they had ensured that he was on the right of the party in 1931. All three factions were in broad agreement about the nature of the Republic. They believed it to be a bourgeois democratic regime which would carry out a classic bourgeois democratic revolution as a first step on Spain's road to progress and ultimately socialism.

The tactical conclusions that the three groups drew from this common central analysis were significantly different. Besteiro adopted the theoretically consistent position that the socialists should leave the bourgeoisie to carry out its own revolution and thereby avoid the danger of letting the working class be used as cannon fodder to defend bourgeois positions. Prieto believed that the socialists had no choice but to collaborate with the republicans, since the establishment of democratic rights was an urgent necessity in itself and because he was convinced that the bourgeoisie was too weak to carry out its own revolution without assistance. Largo Caballero was initially also in favour of collaboration, albeit largely because of the material benefits which he believed would accrue to the socialist movement in general and to the UGT in particular.[9] The fact that the assumption on which these conclusions were based was erroneous was to lead to traumatic division within the socialist movement. The Besteiristas were able to withdraw even deeper into abstentionism and the Caballeristas were driven into a frenzied rhetorical revolutionism which brought devastating consequences in its wake. Only Prieto's sensible pragmatism was capable of producing a valid response to the problems of socialism in the Republic.

The socialist belief that the old Spain was about to be transformed into a modern bourgeois society was based on two mistaken, albeit understandable notions. The first was that the Republican politicians themselves somehow constituted the 'bourgeoisie' about to undertake an historic mission. In fact, they were no more than petty bourgeois intellectuals who were the political and legal servants of the economically powerful oligarchies, both urban and rural. The second was the belief that Spain was still a feudal country and that the great *latifundistas* or landlords of the big estates were like feudal barons. This was comprehensible because of the ramshackle nature of Spanish agriculture and of the semi-feudal social relations pertaining in the countryside between landlords and the landless day labourers, the *braceros* and *jornaleros*, and especially in the treatment of women. In fact, feudalism, in economic and legal terms, had been swept aside during the complex *desamortización* or disentailment processes of the 1830s and 1850s. The urban bourgeoisie and the rural oligarchy had been fused; the urge to make a bourgeois political revolution was neutralised by the attractions of cheap land in terms of both profit and social status. The consequence was that Spain was a backward agrarian country but none the less an agrarian capitalist one.[10]

It is easy now, in the 1980s, armed with the work of a magnificent generation of Spanish economic historians, to see the nineteenth century in such terms. For the socialists in 1930s, it was a different matter. Accordingly, their interpretation of the country's recent past led to tactical conclusions which were to have dramatic consequences. While Besteiro was to withdraw into quietism, Largo Caballero and his youthful followers rejected the entire notion of bourgeois democracy in a perverse misunderstanding of the true relation of forces in 1930s Spain. Their theoretical rejection of the bourgeois Republic was based on resentment that the republicans themselves had failed to fulfil the historic role that had been attributed to them. Prieto took the whole problem more phlegmatically and more realistically. He had expected less and was therefore less disappointed. In contrast, Largo Caballero, as Minister of Labour from 1931 to 1933, had been in the front line of the fiercest class war taking place in the Republic, that between the landless *braceros* and the *latifundistas*.[11] Moreover, because of his position within the UGT and the Agrupación Socialista Madrileña, he was acutely sensitive to the problems of the young, unskilled workers in Madrid who were being radicalised by their social conditions in the industrial suburbs and by pressure from anarchist and communist rivals.[12] Prieto, although fully aware of the hostility of the economic elites to the Republic, had as Minister of Finance – and even more so as Minister of Public Works – a sense that the Republic was able to make positive advances in modernising Spain.[13]

In general, however, the socialists had good reason to feel betrayed and deceived by their collaboration with the republicans. They had decided in 1931 on such a course in the hope of being able to push through significant social reform. They had cooperated to the limit of their possibilities, consistently maintaining trade union discipline under the most provocative circumstances and undergoing the opprobrium of being associated with a government which was seen to use the forces of order against the working class. After the scandal caused by the repression of the minor anarchist uprising at Casas Viejas in January 1933, collaboration was subjected to hostile scrutiny because the reforming hopes of the Republican–Socialist coalition, in the name of which the sacrifices had been made, had not been fulfilled. The failure of reform was largely a consequence of the success with which the Right organised itself to block change – by means of parliamentary obstruction at a national level, and by the use of force at a local level.[14]

Nevertheless, the socialists had some reason to believe that lack of republican commitment to reform had contributed to the right-wing success. Largo Caballero was especially bitter about the behaviour in the Cortes of the group of influential intellectuals loosely gathered together as the Agrupación al Servicio de la República. Elected on the socialist ticket, they had not hesitated to use their seats in parliament to give well-publicised vent to flights of anti-socialist rhetoric in the Cortes. The most influential was the philosopher José Ortega y Gasset (deputy for Leon). Other ASR parliamentary deputies, including Justino de Azcárate (Leon), Antonio Sacristán Colás (Cáceres) and Alfonso García Valdecasas (Granada) were active in the rightist organisation, Frente Español, which was a forerunner of the Falange, although only García Valdecasas was to travel the full distance to fascism.[15] One of the most prominent ASR deputies, José Pareja Yébenes (Granada), joined the Radical Party and others ran in the 1933 elections as independents of the centre. Considerable as was Largo Caballero's distress at this betrayal, it was more than equalled by his bitterness at the Radicals.[16]

At a local level, members of the socialist rural union, the Federación Nacional de Trabajadores de la Tierra, were embittered by the fact that the civil governors of many provinces were displaying little energy in preventing the local *caciques* from simply ignoring government legislation and even less in ensuring that the Civil Guard did not continue to side with landowners in defiance of the spirit of the law.[17] Many of the officials concerned had been appointed when Niceto Alcalá Zamora was Prime Minister and Miguel Maura was Minister of the Interior and were, to say the least, of fairly conservative leanings. Others were Radicals or Radical Socialists who were most unsuitable in terms of their ideological leanings or personal honesty.[18]

Azaña himself was aware of the lack of reforming zeal among many of the Republic's important functionaries.[19] However, that was insufficient to dispel a widespread feeling within the socialist movement that the republicans in general, irrespective of their party, were not very interested in major issues of social reform and were usually unaware of the technical problems involved in getting legislation which had passed through the Cortes made effective in the countryside. This feeling was especially acute in the area of agrarian reform, largely as a result of the punctiliously legalistic delaying tactics of Felipe Sánchez Román at the head of the Comisión Técnica Agraria and Ramón Feced as Director del Instituto de Reforma Agraria. Sánchez Román came to be regarded by the socialists as the principal obstruction to agrarian reform within the republican camp. Even his friends regarded him as one of the most reactionary figures of the Republic.[20] It is hardly surprising, under the circumstances, that there was considerable distrust of the republicans within the socialist ranks. In the eyes of the *El Obrero de la Tierra*, the official newspaper of the UGT's powerful rural labourers' union, the Federación Nacional de Trabajadores de la Tierra, the Radicals and the members of the Acción Republicana were the worst enemies of the Republic. The reason for this was simply that republicanism had no genuine rural base and often it was infiltrated by members of the agrarian bourgeoisie who thereby hoped to legitimise their own social and economic positions. The consequent socialist resentment became acute throughout 1933 with the Radicals taking a prominent role in obstructing government business.

In fact, given the anti-socialist feelings of the Radicals and the ASR, there was every reason for the PSOE, despite disappointments over reform, to cling to its left republican allies. The socialist error in breaking the 1931 electoral coalition made possible the period of the politics of revenge and reprisal, the so-called *bienio negro*, wherein the immediate origins of the civil war are properly to be sought. There was an element of irresponsibility about the decision to go it alone in the 1933 elections. The sweeping victory of the Left in the June 1931 elections had been secured by a coalition which represented the great anti-monarchical Pact of San Sebastián of 1930, comprising the PSOE, the various left republican parties and a great pot-pourri of centre and right-wing republicans including the Radical Party under Alejandro Lerroux. Since Lerroux and many influential rightist republicans had turned violently against the socialists as early as December 1931, the forces of the Left were already at a major disadvantage by comparison with 1931. At best, they faced a three-way fight between themselves, the newly resurgent Right and the Radicals; at worst, an alliance between the Right and the Radicals might stand against them. In those circumstances, to advocate the division of the PSOE and the left republicans, as Largo Caballero did in the autumn of 1933, could only seem frivolous.

However, Largo Caballero was generally embittered by the slowness of reform and particularly enraged by the behaviour of certain prominent republicans. Accordingly, he let himself be carried to the point of a blanket denunciation of all republicans. Moreover, when the PSOE executive committee circularised the local *agrupaciones* for their opinions about collaboration with the republicans in the November 1933 elections, the majority replied that there should be no cooperation. Until the last moment, Prieto maintained the hope that it might be possible to bring about a change of mind in Largo Caballero. When that proved to be impossible, he did the only thing possible to him, which was to include both Azaña and the Radical–Socialist leader nearest to the PSOE, Marcelino Domingo, in the socialist electoral list presented for Vizcaya.[21] The consequences of the decision not to form an electoral coalition with those parties of the republican Left prepared to do so, are well known. Combined with anarchist abstentions, it had the effect, in an electoral system which favoured large coalitions, of giving victory to the Right. The appalling impact on the working-class movement of that victory was at the heart of the popular desire in 1935 to rebuild the Republican–Socialist coalition in order to 'recuperate' the 'real' Republic associated with the period 1931–33.

The results nationally were a disaster for both the PSOE and the left republicans. After gaining 116 seats in the 1931 elections, the PSOE representation in the Cortes now dropped to 58. The left republicans, that is to say Acción Republicana, the Radical Socialists, Esquerra Catalana and the Organización Regional Gallega Autónoma, fell from their 1931 total of 139 deputies to a mere 40.[22] There were numerous places where a united front of socialists and left republicans would almost certainly have ensured left-wing victory – Asturias, Alicante, Badajoz, Ciudad Real, Cordoba, Granada, Jaen, Murcia, to name simply the most clear-cut cases. Moreover, a united front would have ensured such a victory after the first round of the elections, thereby depriving the Radical Party of the temptation and the opportunity to ally with the parties of the Right in the second round, something they did with great success in many southern provinces.[23]

The left republicans were virtually wiped off the electoral map and the socialists had far fewer deputies than their numerical vote seemed to them to justify. Their 1 627 472 votes had given them 58 deputies, while the 806 340 votes gained by the Radicals had secured them 104 seats.[24] Although this was the consequence in part of the socialists' failure to utilise an electoral system which they had helped to elaborate, it was taken as further proof of the falsity of bourgeois democracy. For a variety of reasons, the Socialist Party now took a dramatic turn to the left. To bitterness about the paucity of thorough-going social reform between 1931 and 1933 was added a fear that the socialist rank-and-file might pass to the more militant CNT or the Communist Party if its radicalisation did not find some echo among the PSOE leadership. Above all, there was hope that verbal revolutionism might frighten the Right into moderating its assault on those social advances which the Republic had made, or else scare the President into calling new elections. Such rhetorical extremism could only accelerate the political polarisation set in motion by the distorted electoral results. Moreover, the radicalisation of the socialist movement was to be exploited skilfully by the Right in order to permit the progressive repression of various sections of it throughout 1934. Strike after strike was provoked and section after section of the UGT was emasculated.[25] Prieto opposed the revolutionary line, yet out of loyalty to the Socialist Party, he fulfilled his role more thoroughly than many allegedly convinced revolutionaries. While Prieto drew up plans for a post-revolution government and made abortive arrangements for arms purchases, the burden of rebuilding the Republican–Socialist coalition fell upon Azaña.

It was an enormous task which was to see him imprisoned, publicly vilified and involved in a political campaign in which, against his inclinations, he was to address hundreds of thousands of people. Despite a widespread belief to the contrary, Manuel Azaña was not a personally ambitious man. His first response to being out of power was a sense of relief at being able to return to his books and to escape from the aridity of politics.[26] His withdrawal into private life was in part a reaction to the realisation that it would be difficult to overcome the hostility of the left-wing of the PSOE towards the republicans. In general, Azaña was regarded as an exception within the general socialist perspective of contempt for the republican betrayal, guilty of no more than what Largo Caballero's intellectual spokesman, Luis Araquistain, called 'Azaña's noble error, his beautiful republican utopia of thinking that it was possible to construct and then rule over a state which was not a class state'.[27] Nevertheless, there was considerable tension between the left-wing socialists and Azaña. In 1937, he wrote in his diary: 'I was still on good terms with some socialists, like Prieto, Besteiro, Fernando de los Ríos and others who had always been my friends. I also still had popularity among the masses as was shown by the public meetings that I called. It was a popularity and prestige which did not go down well among the pontiffs of revolutionary extremism. But the "Caballerista" tendency which dominated the PSOE was hostile.'[28]

Accordingly, Azaña's efforts in early 1934 were confined to attempts to facilitate the regrouping of left republican forces and to warn those socialists with whom he had contact that the PSOE's rhetorically revolutionary line could lead to disaster. Azaña was fully aware of the need to rebuild the Republican–Socialist coalition. On 30 September 1932, in a speech to the Acción Republicana branch in Santander, he had declared:

> I believe, I say it here and I will repeat it wherever it is necessary, that I do not know if the presence of the socialists in the government brings them benefit or not; the question is of no interest to me. The presence of the socialists in the government, and I repeat it, has been one of the most important services – so important that it was unavoidable – that they could ever have given the republican regime.[29]

Azaña's awareness of the need for Republican–Socialist collaboration was strengthened by the disaster of November 1933. Even before the elections, he had hinted at the catastrophic consequences of going divided into the electoral contest.[30] After Prieto made the public announcement of the termination of the Republican–Socialist coalition, Azaña declared in the Cortes on 2 October 1933:

> the government is finished, our collaboration is finished; you are taking another road, we are continuing down the road of the republicans, but between us there will always remain the invisible bridge of the emotions experienced in common and of the service given to the Spanish fatherland.[31]

Now, in early 1934, realising that there was little possibility of overcoming Largo Caballero's distrust, Azaña confined himself to the immediately urgent and realisable tasks of restructuring the shattered republican camp and giving sound advice to those socialists who would listen.

Azaña was fully informed of the socialist belief that threats of revolution might restrain the Radical–CEDA coalition through messages from Prieto passed to him by Marcelino Domingo and through his own direct contacts with Fernando de los Ríos. With the permission of the PSOE executive committee, de los Ríos had passed on to him a copy of the socialists' proposal for revolutionary action. On 2 January 1934, Azaña informed de los Ríos in extremely strong language that an uprising was condemned to be smashed by the army and that it was the duty of the socialist leadership to control the impulses of the rank-and-file. 'I said terrible things to him', Azaña noted in his diary, 'I don't know how he put up with them.' Although de los Ríos was personally moved by what Azaña had said and passed it on to other members of the socialist executive, it had little effect.[32] Given the ferocity of the rightist attacks on the working class, even Prieto was in no mood to listen to reason and almost certainly seduced by the possibility of revolutionary action. Years later, speaking in the Círculo Pablo Iglesias in Mexico City, he said:

> I declare myself guilty before my own conscience, before the Socialist Party and before the whole of Spain, for my participation in that revolutionary movement. I declare it as guilt, as sin, not as glory. I am free of blame for the genesis of that movement, but I must take full responsibility for its preparation and development . . . I accepted tasks from which others fled because there hung over them the risk not only of losing their liberty but the more painful shadow of losing their honour. Nevertheless, I undertook those tasks. I collaborated in that movement heart and soul, I accepted the aforementioned tasks and I found myself violently outraged.[33]

The painfulness of Prieto's position was quickly perceived by Azaña.

Azaña had taken the opportunity of coinciding with Prieto in Barcelona during the campaign for the Catalan municipal elections to renew his warnings about the dangers of continued left-wing disunity. This was the theme of his speech in the Barcelona bull ring on 7 January, but it seems to have had little effect on Prieto with whom he lunched on the following day at the Font del Lleó.[34] Nevertheless, Azaña continued to try to re-establish contact with the socialists. On 4 February, Prieto, appalled by the rightist onslaught against the working class, went along with the Caballeristas and threatened that a revolutionary uprising would take place. Exactly seven days later, Azaña, speaking, as did Prieto in the Pardiñas Theatre in Madrid, made a monumental speech warning against the frivolous resort to revolutionary solutions, but also recognising how the government's contempt for social justice was provoking the socialists. It was a reasoned appeal for unity and moderation, but the socialists were not yet ready to pay heed to him.[35]

Azaña had rather more success in his self-appointed task of attempting to unify the fragmented and demoralised left republican parties. His hope was that 'from the remains of three small parties, there would emerge a nucleus already possessing a certain importance by the mere fact of the merger and which would have strength and authority to attract many other republicans and to grow rapidly'. After overcoming petty rivalries and distrust between the groups, Azaña secured on 2 April 1934 the unification of Marcelino Domingo's Partido Radical Socialista Independiente, Santiago Casares Quiroga's Organización Regional

Gallega Autónoma and his own Acción Republicana into the Izquierda Republicana.[36] Azaña became the new party's president and Marcelino Domingo its vice-president. While the formation of Izquierda Republicana did not lead to the reunification of the entire republican camp, it did begin a major process of rationalisation. When the liberal wing of the Radical Party broke away from Lerroux in May 1934 under the leadership of Diego Martínez Barrio, it was not long before it was in contact with the rump of the Radical Socialist Party of Félix Gordón Ordás which had been left somewhat isolated by the union of Domingo and Azaña. Negotiations throughout the summer of 1934 led to the foundation on 11 September of the Unión Republicana.[37] This was to facilitate considerably Azaña's plans for a broad concentration of the moderate Left.

The other front of Azaña's activities – relations with the socialists – was not progressing so smoothly. In a desultory fashion, the PSOE revolutionary committee, organised by Largo Caballero, played at making preparations for the forthcoming rising. The sheer unreality of the committee's activities suggests that Caballero, at least, hoped that it would never be necessary to put its plans to the test. Prieto, against the hostility of Largo Caballero, tried on a number of occasions throughout 1934 to have Azaña and Domingo apprised of the preparations being made. Perhaps Prieto hoped to subject Largo Caballero to the cold reason which Azaña would inevitably have brought to the proceedings. However, at a joint meeting of the executive committees of the PSOE and the UGT in mid-March 1934, Largo declared that there would be no collaboration with the republicans either in the revolutionary movement or in the subsequent provisional government.[38]

It was hardly surprising that when Azaña made an initiative for renewed Republican–Socialist collaboration in June he should be rebuffed by Largo Caballero. The meeting took place at the home of José Salmerón, secretary general of Izquierda Republicana. Salmerón, Marcelino Domingo and Azaña represented their party. Largo Caballero, Enrique de Francisco and a third socialist (probably Vidarte who was, like de Francisco, one of the revolutionary committee's secretaries) represented the PSOE. Azaña spoke for an hour about the need for unity and the profound effect that the announcement of such unity would have on the political situation. Azaña was absolutely right. The CEDA leader, Gil Robles had already begun his very successful tactic of periodically withdrawing support from the Radicals in order to provoke cabinet crises and thus a gradual break-up of Lerroux's party. At each crisis, when consulted by the president of the Republic, Azaña recommended a dissolution of the Cortes and the calling of elections.

There would have been far more chance of Alcalá Zamora agreeing, and thereby resolving the acute problems of the day without violence, if there had existed a united block of left republican and socialist forces. Largo Caballero, however, was not interested and said that he had attended the meeting merely 'out of personal deference to those who had called it'. In the hope that circumstances might change, Azaña concluded the meeting with a formula which left the door open to future contacts: 'each would develop his thoughts in case circumstances required their modification'.[39]

Largo Caballero declared at that meeting that he could not be seen by the socialist masses to be entering into an agreement with the republicans for fear of being 'materially and morally diminished'. Largo's determination to be seen to be as militant as his UGT rank-and-file was the greatest obstacle to Azaña's plans for rebuilding the Republican–Socialist coalition. That he was fully aware of this had been made clear in his great speech 'Grandeurs and Servitudes of Politics' given in the Bilbao liberal club *El Sitio* on 21 April 1934. In it, he had warned, with an eye to the provocatively revolutionary lines being followed by the PSOE and the Catalan republicans of the Esquerra Catalana, against the dangers of being carried along by the crowd.[40] Largo Caballero's remarks at the meeting held in Salmerón's house suggested that Azaña's warnings had been ignored. However, at the end of September, Don Manuel made one last try to get the socialists to see reason. On 26 September 1934, Jaime Carner, the wealthy Catalan republican who had been Azaña's Minister of Finance, died. Azaña went to the funeral along with numerous other republican figures. In fact, he had been in Barcelona less than a month previously and had made a speech calling for the reconquest of the Republic. Now, at the end of September, coinciding again with Prieto and de los Ríos at the Font del Lleó, Azaña lamented the lack of agreement between the socialists and the left republicans.

The realism of what Azaña had to say could hardly affect the position of either Prieto or de los Ríos since they were unable to influence attitudes within a PSOE dominated by Caballero and the militant youth. As Azaña himself noted:

> Prieto maintained a stony silence throughout the entire discussion. All that we said probably seemed otiose to him, and perhaps he was right. I was sure that Prieto did not approve of the plans for armed insurrection but that he was going along with [them] out of fatalism, out of a belief that they were unstoppable, out of party discipline.[41]

Accordingly, when three ministers of the CEDA entered the cabinet on 4 October, the ill-prepared rising broke out in Madrid, Catalonia and Asturias. At one level, this represented the defeat of Azaña's efforts to bring the Spanish Left to reason. At another, by galvanising Prieto into joining him in a quest for a great electoral union of the Left, it constituted the starting point for his greatest triumph: the Popular Front.

The impact of Asturias on the PSOE and the UGT was catastrophic – imprisonment and torture for many militants, exile for others, the closing of Casas del Pueblo, the harassment of trade unions and the silencing of the socialist press. From this disaster, the Prietista and the Caballerista wings of the movement drew entirely different conclusions. Caballero, advised by members of the radicalised Socialist Youth, with whom he was imprisoned, and several of whom, including Santiago Carrillo, were later to join the PCE, concluded that an even more revolutionary line should be adopted. Prieto argued much more rationally that the first priority was to regain power in order to put an end to the sufferings of the working class at the hands of the governing Radical–CEDA coalition. Prieto was able to take this stand with enormous authority because, whereas the revolutionary movement had been a fiasco in the areas controlled by the Caballerista Youth, the most effective action by the workers had taken place precisely in those regions dominated by Prietistas – Asturias and the Basque Country. Moreover, since the 'Bolshevisers' denied, not without reason, their participation in the events of October, they virtually handed the legacy of the movement to Prieto.

Throughout 1935, Prieto was to use that legacy to try to secure working-class backing for the initiatives made by Azaña. Azaña himself had been arrested in Barcelona at the beginning of the October events and imprisoned until the end of December 1934. Subjected to vilification by the right-wing press, he became a symbol for all those in Spain who were suffering from the authoritarian politics of the Radical–CEDA coalition. Intensely embittered by the experience – as is illustrated by his book *Mi rebelión en Barcelona* – Azaña was inspired by the popular support that he received during his persecution to redouble his efforts for the recuperation of the Republic. His release coincided with his Saint's day and Izquierda Republicana invited all those who sympathised with him to send a card or telegram of congratulations. The messages of support arrived at the party's Madrid headquarters by the hundreds of thousands. A member of the Izquierda Republicana Youth described the scene:

the postmen could not cope with the delivery of the cards and telegrams, bearing bulging postal sacks for which there was soon no room in the party's branch offices. An endless queue of citizens, both men and women, endlessly delivered their personal congratulations and wound around the block, through the Puerta del Sol and down the Calle del Arenal. That spontaneous demonstration of hope by the Madrileños and from Spaniards from the furthest confines of the country was a surprise for all of us, even the initiators of the idea.[42]

Azaña was clearly moved by this demonstration of popular esteem and what he took to be enthusiasm for a return to the Republic of 1931–33. He wrote to Prieto on 16 January 1935:

a movement of optimism and hope has been produced here, simply by the fact of my liberation, and for that reason I have been the object of an almost plebiscitary demonstration by all the forces and organisations of the Left in Spain.[43]

While urging Prieto to work for the creation of a political alliance which would allow the winning of the next elections, Azaña himself worked to consolidate the republican unification begun in the previous spring. In the late summer of 1934, he had used his influence to ensure that the new party Unión Republicana would drop its anti-socialist leanings. After his release from prison, he renewed his contacts with Unión Republicana and also with the conservative Felipe Sánchez Román's Partido Nacional Republicano. This bore fruit in the joint declaration issued on 12 April 1935 listing the minimum conditions which they regarded as essential for the reconstruction of political coexistence in Spain. The seven conditions were: the prevention of torture of political prisoners; the re-establishment of constitutional guarantees; the release of those imprisoned for the events of October 1934; an end to discrimination against left-wing and liberal functionaries; the readmission to their jobs of workers dismissed after the October strike; the legal existence of trade unions and the reinstatement of the town councils overthrown by the government.[44] This programme was the potential basis of a renewal of the Republican–Socialist coalition.

In order to achieve the implementation of these conditions, an electoral victory was clearly essential and the repression after October had imposed sufficient realism on many of the Left to make it a viable prospect. On the basis of this minimal agreement, Azaña and Prieto worked together to recreate the electoral coalition. From his exile,

Prieto's crucial task was to seek areas of agreement between the republican camp and moderate socialists and, even more importantly, to neutralise the irresponsible extremism of the Caballeristas, which inevitably earned him their virulent hostility.[45] Azaña's role was even more crucial. It consisted of the massive effort of publicity and propaganda which not only took the idea of a resuscitated electoral coalition to hundreds of thousands of Spaniards, but also, more crucially, demonstrated to the left wing of the PSOE the immense popular support that there existed for an electoral agreement.

Azaña's campaign of *discursos en campo abierto*, or open-air speeches, began on 26 May at the Campo de Mestalla in Valencia. Before more than 100 000 spectators, he announced that Izquierda Republicana was working with other parties on an electoral platform and a future plan of government which would eventually be submitted to the approval of groups further to the left. Then on 14 July, he spoke to an even larger crowd at the Campo de Lasesarre in Baracaldo near Bilbao, provoking intense enthusiasm when he called for new elections and defended the necessity of an electoral coalition. However, the culmination and the most spectacular event of his campaign came on 20 October 1935 at Comillas, on what in those days were the outskirts of Madrid. Azaña was thoroughly aware of the wider implications of his campaign. On the day before he was due to speak, he visited Comillas by car and somewhat surprised by the size of the venue asked the members of the organising committee, 'Do you really think that this will be filled? Because if not, we are going to look ridiculous.' In the event nearly half a million people arrived to hear him elaborate his projected programme of government.[46] The English journalist Henry Buckley wrote of the occasion:

> More than half the spectators could not even see the stand from which the former Prime Minister addressed them. The loudspeakers functioned only partially and therefore tens of thousands not only saw nothing but they heard nothing either. This meeting had not been widely advertised. It was frowned upon by the authorities and in some cases the Civil Guard turned back convoys of trucks carrying spectators. All vehicles bringing people from afar were stopped some miles outside Madrid, thus causing endless confusion and forcing weary men and women to trudge a long distance after a tiring ride. Admission was by payment. The front seats cost twelve shillings and sixpence and the cheaper ones ten shillings and half a crown. Standing room at the back cost sixpence. No one was forced to go to that meeting. Presence there, in fact, was much more likely to bring the

displeasure of employer or landlord . . . From the furthest points of
Spain there were groups who had travelled in some cases six hundred
miles in rainy cold weather in open motor lorries.[47]

At the end of speech, Azaña called the huge crowd to total silence and
ended with the moving words:

> The silence of the people declares its grief and indignation; but the
> voice of the people can sound as terrifying as the trumpets of the day
> of judgement. Let my words not rebound against frivolous hearts but
> penetrate yours like darts of fire. People, for Spain and for the
> Republic, unite!

His listeners burst into a frenetic ovation and thousands of clenched fists
flowered. Azaña did not return the salute.[48] Like the sorcerer's
apprentice, the mild liberal politician was taken aback by the fervour of
proletarian passion. It was a prophetic moment which perhaps presaged
Azaña's withdrawal into isolation during the civil war. None the less,
not only did the display of discipline by those who attended seriously
disturb the Right, but the sheer size of the crowd and its enthusiasm
helped resolve remaining doubts among those who still opposed the
creation of the electoral front.

In the meanwhile, the PSOE was in turmoil over the future electoral
tactics to be adopted. The first initiatives came from Prieto. He had been
in correspondence on the subject with Azaña since late 1934. His ideas
were shared by the party secretary Juan-Simeón Vidarte who visited the
Cárcel Modelo in the middle of March 1935 to put them to Largo
Caballero. Largo was as hostile as ever to the idea of a coalition but he
authorised Vidarte to ask Prieto to outline his ideas more fully. This he
did, and Prieto wrote a long letter from Paris on 23 March 1935 to be
used as a memorandum for discussion by the PSOE executive committee. He was at pains to point out that the idea of a workers' block
defended by Largo Caballero would almost certainly lead to a repetition
of the electoral defeat of November 1933. Instead, Prieto advocated 'a
circumstantial alliance that should extend to our left and to our right'.
For Prieto, the key issue was to ensure a vote which would put an end to
the abuses committed by the Radical–CEDA coalition and that was
unlikely with an exclusively proletarian alliance. In fact, there was no
guarantee of working-class unity given the anarchists' suspicions of
what they saw as socialist imperialism. Prophetically, Prieto also
pointed out that to hitch the wagon of the PSOE to the horses of the PCE
and the CNT would be dangerous. On the basis of Prieto's letter, Vidarte

drew up a circular which was widely distributed within the socialist movement. It led to intense debate and finally revealed a considerable rank-and-file majority in favour of concrete action to put an end to the rule of Gil Robles and Lerroux.[49]

On 31 March 1935, Prieto had received a letter from Ramón González Peña, the hero of Asturias, supporting his position.[50] Confident that important sectors of the party were with him, Prieto published an article on 14 April 1935 in his paper *El Liberal* calling for socialist collaboration with the broad front of republicans being forged by Azaña and Martínez Barrio. His argument was overwhelming: another electoral victory for Gil Robles would mean the end of democracy in Spain. Although these views struck a chord in the hearts of the rank-and-file who had suffered the daily brutality of life under the Radical–CEDA coalition, they infuriated the 'Bolshevising' Socialist Youth. Attacks were launched on Prieto by Carlos Hernández Zancajo, Santiago Carrillo and Amaro del Rosal in the form of the pamphlet *Octubre – segunda etapa*, published in April, and by Carlos de Baraibar, in the form of a book entitled *Las falsas 'posiciones socialistas' de Indalecio Prieto*, published in June. This was a reply to a pamphlet by Prieto entitled *Del momento: posiciones socialistas* which collected together five of his articles originally published in *El Liberal* of Bilbao, *La Libertad* of Madrid and several provincial republican newspapers. Together, the five articles constituted a reasoned defence of the need for an electoral alliance. His pamphlet enjoyed far wider distribution and far deeper influence than the rather insubstantial polemic of Baraibar. As far as the Caballeristas were concerned, Prieto was working to save a doomed bourgeois democracy. Prieto understood why they felt disappointed by the Republic, but he had a far more realistic view of the real relation of forces in Spain. The strength of the oligarchy was such as to make threats of revolution seem utopian. Thus, for Prieto, it was essential in the uneven fight between the oligarchy and the workers that the workers at least have the machinery of the state on their side. The repressive policies of the Radical–CEDA government had ensured that the revolutionary rhetoric of the Caballeristas had found an echo among the rank-and-file. Even more, however, the memory of the Asturian October, the continued existence of thousands of political prisoners, and the desire to remove Gil Robles and Lerroux ensured a sympathetic mass response to Prieto's call for unity and a return to the progressive Republic of 1931–33.

With Prieto still in exile, the job of carrying the call to the masses was undertaken by Azaña. On 7 August, three weeks after his huge public meeting at Baracaldo, replete with *Vivas!* for Prieto, Azaña wrote to him: 'I believe that you have won the day, not only as far as public opinion is concerned but also within the mass of your own party. This is not just my opinion but also of many people, socialists and non-socialists.'[51] The theoretical polemics of the PSOE Left had little impact on the rank-and-file and Prieto continued to work confidently for union, meeting Azaña in Belgium in mid-September to discuss the programme of the projected coalition. On 14 November 1935, Azaña wrote formally to Enrique de Francisco of the PSOE executive committee proposing and electoral understanding.[52] Impelled by the evidence of the popular support enjoyed by Azaña in his campaign of *discursos en campo abierto* and by the change of tactics adopted by their communist allies, the Caballeristas came round to Prieto's point of view.

A complex process of negotiation over the Popular Front programme remained – carried forward by Amos Salvador of Izquierda Republicana, Bernardo Giner de los Ríos of Unión Republicana and Manuel Cordero and Juan-Simeón Vidarte for the UGT and PSOE and in representation of the other working-class groups.[53] The adherence of Largo Caballero would not have been possible without the efforts of the communists. They were fully aware of the hostility felt towards them by Azaña and Prieto and were anxious to see Largo Caballero join the Front not least because his preference for a more proletarian union would guarantee their presence. Accordingly, they worked hard to get him to drop his opposition, even sending Jacques Duclos to try to persuade him. Nevertheless, the fact remains that the core of the Popular Front was the Republican–Socialist electoral coalition recreated by the efforts of Azaña and Prieto. No one, however, not even Prieto, worked harder than Azaña to ensure the electoral success of the Spanish Left in February 1936. Indeed, if anything swayed the doubting Largo Caballero, it was almost certainly the evidence of popular endorsement for the idea of union displayed during Azaña's propaganda campaign. The victory of the Popular Front was ultimately the victory of Manuel Azaña, born both of his diplomacy behind the scenes and his massive popularity in the country as a whole.

Notes

1. Letter of Azaña to Prieto, 20 April 1935, Manuel Azaña, *Obras completas*, volume III (Mexico DF, 1966–68) p. 602; Juan-Simeón Vidarte, *El bienio negro y la insurrección de Asturias* (Barcelona, 1978) pp. 494–5.

2. Joaquín Arrarás, preface to Manuel Azaña, *Memorias íntimas de Azaña* (Madrid, 1939) p. 6.
3. Francisco Casares, *Azaña y ellos* (Granada, 1938) pp. 26, 34.
4. Cf. Paul Preston, *The Coming of the Spanish Civil War* (London, 1978) pp. 92–122, 151–68.
5. Joaquín Arrarás, *Historia de la cruzada española*, volume 2 (Madrid, 1939–43) p. 423.
6. Joaquín Arrarás, *Historia de la segunda República española*, volume 4 (Madrid, 1956–68) p. 17.
7. Dolores Ibárruri, *El único camino* (Paris, 1965) pp. 215–19, 223–5; *Guerra y revolución en España 1936–1939* volume 1 (Moscow, 1967–77) pp. 66–78. Cf. Joaquín Maurín, *Revolución y contrarrevolución en España* (Paris, 1966) p. 286.
8. Gabriel Jackson presented the Popular Front as the result of the coincidence of two impulses, that of Azaña and that of the Comintern, in *The Spanish Republic and the Civil War 1931–1939* (Princeton, 1965) pp. 185–7. An extremely complete account of the genesis of the Popular Front in terms of those two currents was provided by Ricardo de la Cierva, *Historia de la guerra civil española: perspectivas y antecedentes 1898–1936* (Madrid, 1969) pp. 579–610. Santos Juliá, *Orígenes del Frente Popular en España (1934–1936)* (Madrid, 1969) *passim* and especially pp. 27–41, is an account giving the fullest attention to Azaña's role and is the clearest account to date of the complex process whereby the electoral unity of 1936 was so laboriously created. The view which presents the Popular Front as something created during rapid negotiations carried out in the week following the publication on 7 January 1936 of the decree calling elections is no longer tenable. Cf. Stanley G. Payne, *The Spanish Revolution* (London, 1970) pp. 176–8.
9. On the divisions within the PSOE, see Preston, *The Coming of the Spanish Civil War*, pp. 5–24.
10. Paul Preston, 'Spain' in Stuart Woolf, (ed.), *Fascism in Europe* (London, 1981).
11. Paul Preston, 'The Agrarian War in the South', in Paul Preston (ed.) *Revolution and War in Spain 1931–1939* (London, 1984).
12. Santos Juliá, 'Economic Crisis, social conflict and the Popular Front: Madrid 1931–1936', in Preston (ed.) *Revolution and War*.
13. See the Prieto centenary issue of the *Revista del Ministerio de Obras Públicas y Urbanismo* (Madrid) No. 305, December 1983.
14. Preston, *The Coming of the Spanish Civil War*, chapter 2.
15. Francisco Largo Caballero, *Posibilismo socialista en la democracia* (Madrid, 1934) *passim*; Francisco Largo Caballero, *Mis recuerdos* (Mexico DF, 1954) p. 129; Vidarte, *El bienio negro*, p. 20; Ian Gibson, *En busca de José Antonio* (Barcelona, 1980) p. 59; Sheelagh Ellwood, *Prietas las filas: Historia de Falange Española, 1933–1983* (Barcelona, 1984) pp. 36–8.
16. Caballero, *Mis recuerdos*, p. 129; unpublished autobiography, 'Notas históricas de la guerra en España, 1917–1940', (manuscript held in the archives of the Fundación Pablo Iglesias, Madrid) pp. 15–16.
17. *El Obrero de la Tierra*, 14, 28 January, 25 February 1933.
18. *El Socialista*, 5 March 1932; Miguel Maura, *Así cayó Alfonso XIII* (Barcelona, 1966) pp. 265–72.

19. Azaña, *Obras*, volume IV, pp. 644, 648.
20. Juan-Simeón Vidarte, *Las Cortes Constituyentes de 1931–1933* (Barcelona, 1976) pp. 471–8; Azaña, *Memorias íntimas*, pp. 90–3; Edward E. Malefakis, *Agrarian Reform and Peasant Revolution in Spain* (New Haven, 1970) pp. 243–57, 389.
21. Vidarte, *El bienio negro*, p. 21. See also the minutes of the meetings of the PSOE executive committee, Actas de la Comisión Ejecutiva del PSOE, held at the Fundación Pablo Iglesias, Madrid, 24, 25, 27, 31 October, 22, 29 November 1933.
22. It is difficult to arrive at absolutely accurate party loyalties of deputies in the republican Cortes. Cf. Juan J. Linz, 'The Party System of Spain: Past and Future', in Seymour M. Lipset and Stein Rokkan (eds), *Party Systems and Voter Alignments* (New York, 1967) p. 260; Enrique López Sevilla, *El Partido Socialista en las Cortes Constituyentes de la segunda República* (Mexico, 1969); Jesús Lozano, *La segunda República: imágenes, cronología y documentos* (Barcelona, 1973) pp. 445–62.
23. José María Gil Robles, *No fue posible la paz* (Barcelona, 1968) pp. 102–5.
24. Francisco Largo Caballero, *Discursos a los trabajadores* (Madrid, 1934) pp. 163–6.
25. Preston, *The Coming of the Spanish Civil War*, pp. 92–124.
26. Azaña, *Obras*, volume IV, p. 661. The notion of impersonal and disinterested service to the public good runs throughout Azaña's speeches and writings, both public and private. See his speech in Santander on 20 September 1932, Azaña, *Obras*, volume II, pp. 429–45: 'The head of government, as far as politics is concerned, has no friends and wants none. Friendship ends before politics or else begins after politics.'
27. Luis Araquistain, 'La utopía de Azaña, *Leviatán*, no. 5, September 1934, pp. 18–30.
28. Azaña, *Obras*, volume IV, pp. 643–4.
29. Azaña, *Obras*, volume II, p. 434.
30. Azaña, *Obras*, volume II, pp. 833–42.
31. Azaña, *Obras*, volume II, pp. 849–50.
32. Azaña, *Obras*, volume IV, pp. 649–52; Vidarte, *El bienio negro*, pp. 90–7.
33. Indalecio Prieto, *Discursos en America con el pensamiento puesto en España* (Mexico DF, 1945) pp. 102–3.
34. Azaña, *Obras*, volume IV, pp. 659–60, and volume II, pp. 901–10.
35. *El Liberal*, 6 February 1934; Azaña, *Obras*, volume II, pp. 911–44 and especially pp. 926–7; Vidarte, *El bienio negro*, pp. 98–100.
36. Azaña, *Obras*, volume IV, pp. 660–1.
37. Manuel Ramírez Jiménez, 'La formación de Unión Republicana y su papel en las elecciones de 1936' in *Las reformas de la segunda República* (Madrid, 1977) pp. 125-69.
38. Preston, *The Coming of the Spanish Civil War*, pp. 119–23; Vidarte, *El bienio negro*, pp. 113–14, 141, 184–5, 210; Manuel Benavides, *La revolución fue asi* (Barcelona, 1935) pp. 9–20.
39. Azaña, *Obras*, volume IV, pp. 653–4.
40. Azaña, *Obras*, volume III, pp. 5–21, especially pp. 11–13.
41. Azaña, *Obras*, volume IV, pp. 667–8.
42. A. C. Márquez Tornero, *Testimonio de mi tiempo (memorias de un español*

republicano) (Madrid, 1979) p. 115; Cipriano Rivas Xerif, *Retrato de un desconocido (vida de Manuel Azaña)* (Mexico DF, 1961) p. 225.

43. Azaña, *Obras*, volume III, pp. 591–3.
44. *La Libertad*, 13 April 1935; Diego Martínez Barrio, *Orígenes del Frente Popular español* (Buenos Aires, 1943) pp. 24–31; La Cierva, *Historia*, pp. 585–6; Juliá, *Orígenes del Frente Popular en España*, pp. 31–3.
45. For Prieto's role, see Preston, *The Coming of the Spanish Civil War*, pp. 133–49; Santos Juliá, *La izquierda del PSOE (1935–1936)* (Madrid, 1977) pp. 53–111; Vidarte, *El bienio negro*, pp. 387–514.
46. Azaña, *Obras*, volume III, pp. 229–93; Márquez Tornero, *Testimonio*, pp. 118–21.
47. Henry Buckley, *Life and Death of the Spanish Republic* (London, 1940) pp. 182–3.
48. Frank Sedwick, *The Tragedy of Manuel Azaña and the Fate of the Spanish Republic* (Ohio, 1963) p. 152.
49. Letter from Vidarte to Prieto, 20 March 1935, letters from Prieto to the PSOE executive committee, 23 March and 26 April 1935, *Documentos socialistas* (Madrid, 1935) pp. 17–26.
50. Letter from Ramón González Peña to Prieto, 31 March 1935, and replies by González Peña to a questionnaire sent to him by the Madrid branch of the Socialist Youth Movement, *Documentos socialistas*, pp. 143–55.
51. Letter from Azaña to Prieto, 7 August 1935, Azaña, *Obras*, volume III, pp. 603–4.
52. Letter from Azaña to de Francisco, 14 November 1935, in Fundación Pablo Iglesias, Madrid, (AH, 24–9).
53. Vidarte, *El bienio negro* pp. 493–514; Preston, *The Coming of the Spanish Civil War*, pp. 144–9.

6 The Spanish Popular Front and the Civil War
Helen Graham

The term Popular Front, in the context of Spain before the civil war, is most accurately used to describe the electoral pact which triumphed at the polls on 16 February 1936. The pact was supported by the entire Spanish Left, with the exception of the still apolitical anarchist trade union organisation, the CNT, whose base, nevertheless, voted *en masse* for the Popular Front candidates.[1] However, in that the Left groups' participation was effectively by proxy through the Spanish Socialist Party, the PSOE, which represented all the proletarian political and union groups on the National Committee of the Popular Front that drew up the list of candidates for the electoral alliance in conjunction with the progressive and moderate republican groupings, then a certain continuity can be seen to exist with the Republican–Socialist reformist coalition, then governmental as well as electoral, of the first two years of the Republic.

For the road to the Popular Front in Spain was the converse of the 1934 French prototype of Socialist–Communist alliance extended to include the Radical Party in a wide 'rassemblement populaire'.[2] The germ of the Spanish Popular Front as a project of parliamentary reform is to be found in the Republican–Socialist coalition of 1931–33, although the credibility of this was massively boosted in 1935–36, perhaps even entirely restored, by the huge injection of popular enthusiasm consequent upon the Spanish Communist Party's new-found commitment to an inter-class alliance after the Comintern had floated the Popular Front line at its Seventh Congress in the July and August of 1935.[3]

The government constituted the day after the February electoral triumph was, although termed Popular Front, an entirely republican administration, and this homogeneity was at once both symptom and cause of the abiding internal weakness of the Spanish Popular Front. From its inception it was weakened immeasurably because the PSOE, which ought to have provided the driving force for the programme of social and economic reform, was riven by a violent internal dispute. This internal division ostensibly set reformist socialists or social democrats

106

against the revolutionary wing of the party; that is, it apparently concerned the fundamental tactical debate over roads to socialism: the violent seizure of power by a party of the revolutionary van, or the long march via the institutions of state. In reality, the dispute had much less to do with differences of political doctrine or tactics than it did with organisational rivalries in the socialist movement. However, the net result of the division was chaos and an organisational dislocation of unprecedented dimensions within the party. Because the PSOE should have formed the bedrock of the Popular Front government experiment, this inner division served effectively to prevent the implementation of a genuine reforming option in the crucial period after the February 1936 elections. Had a strong executive power existed then – strong, that is, both in its determination to enact thoroughgoing social and economic reform and to deal severely with the military conspirators – then it is conceivable that the coup of 17–18 July could have been successfully forestalled.

It is by no means an exaggeration to describe the PSOE as the linchpin of the Second Republic as an experiment in social and economic modernisation by means of parliamentary reform and, therefore, equally an essential component in the creation and consolidation of the Spanish Popular Front. The PSOE was the party of the Spanish working class *par excellence*, with a well-established national network, a long tradition of moral austerity, reforming zeal and, most importantly, of parliamentary activity.[4] Given also that all political action was an anathema to the CNT and that, prior to the civil war, the PCE was numerically so slight as to be politically negligible, it is hardly surprising that the weak forces of progressive republicanism, and Manuel Azaña in particular, should in 1931 have looked to the socialist organisation as a natural ally and a source of vital support against the immense forces of the economic oligarchy which would be bound to obstruct any attempt to alter, even minimally, the balance of socio-economic power in Spain.

For the socialists, the value of the Republic was consubstantial with its reforming achievements; as a political form in itself it was worthless. As Indalecio Prieto, the leader of the reformist wing of the party, expounded in his famous statesman's speech at Cuenca on 1 May 1936, the Republic provided a framework for the 'interior conquest' of Spain. By this he meant the modernisation of her social and economic structures and, implying as this did a redistribution of economic power in Spain, inevitably, the destruction of oligarchy by reducing the power of entrenched interest groups such as the *latifundistas* who owned the vast agricultural estates of central and southern Spain.[5]

It is the contention here that Popular Front, such as it was conceived in Spain by progressive republicans and reformist socialists on the basis of the reforming coalition of 1931–33, but with the tremendous injection of novelty afforded by the post-Seventh Congress communist commitment, remained unrealised throughout the spring and summer of 1936, was temporarily aborted as a result of military rising, republican vacillation and popular revolution, and was only genuinely created in May 1937 when, as a consequence of the cabinet crisis which definitively excluded the socialist Left from power, Juan Negrín assumed the premiership of a government such as Prieto had sought, if not fought, to lead a year previously. He assumed control, however, in circumstances which, it hardly needs underlining, were radically different from those which Prieto would have faced. The latter's task would have been to carry forward the social and economic reforms which were, in essence, the *raison d'être* of the Spanish Popular Front, while acting resolutely to liquidate the threat of military coup. Negrín, called upon to lead a wartime government, took up the task of organising the resistance to the nationalist war machine while attempting also to engineer a political or diplomatic resolution of the conflict.

The fundamental objective of the Popular Front experiment in the Spanish context was to ensure the legislation and implementation of a series of reforms, begun in the first period of the Republic between 1931 and 1933, which had largely been aborted during the period of the clerical–conservative government between 1933 and 1935.[6] Of course, the fact that the electoral pact of February 1936 and the subsequent republican government were both denominated Popular Front, reflected an awareness of the increasingly acute international situation, as it did the intense political polarisation occurring within Spain. However, for the republicans and above all for Indalecio Prieto – the reformist socialist most closely associated with the Popular Front – an awareness of political trends abroad and the experience of domestic tensions served only to increase the determination with which the re-enactment of reform was to be pursued.

By the end of 1935, the socialist Left had also accepted the idea of an inter-class electoral pact, if not a repetition of coalition government. This acceptance of the pact is entirely attributable to the Left's characteristic pragmatism. The Caballerista wing, always extremely sensitive to currents emanating from the rank-and-file, reacted to the overwhelming popular demand for a political amnesty to free the many thousands of people imprisoned during the repression after the revolt of the Asturian miners in October 1934.[7] It was also true, of course, that the

PCE, with its policy of embryonic Popular Front expressed as *bloque popular*, had also been attempting to win the socialist Left over to the idea of collaboration with the republicans. However, it was supremely the amnesty demand which focused the enormous popular fervour and enthusiasm that were so much the hallmark of the electoral campaign, as it was also the basis of the very considerable grass-roots support for working-class unity initiatives at the time. A measure of the strength and irresistible appeal of the Popular Front initiative in the context of domestic political polarisation and the advance of fascism internationally, is to be found in the CNT's consistent underplaying of its traditional apoliticism.[8]

The massive popular vote in February and the exhilaration of electoral success, however, could only very temporarily disguise the fundamental contradiction between the intentions of the architects of the pact and the aspirations of the social base of Popular Front.[9] In essence, this was the same tension which had existed between the possibilities of the Republican–Socialist coalition government of 1931–33 and the increasing popular aspiration to more radical reform. By 1936, after a process of political polarisation both nationally and internationally, the tensions were that much more acute. The most obvious manifestation of popular aspirations overflowing the limits of the Popular Front government strategy came in the spring and summer of 1936 with the wave of land occupations in the south. Later, of course – and more dramatically – it would be this social base of the Popular Front which, across party and labour organisation divisions, would come to the fore as the constructor of the revolutionary organs of parallel power which substituted the paralysed institutions of state in the days and months following the military rising of 18 July.

The convergence over Popular Front was also instrumental in effecting the rapprochement of reformist socialists and the PCE whose basic policy lines over the constitution and objectives of the Popular Front were the same.[10] It was Prieto's private conviction that the heterogenous electoral pact was peripheral to the real issue, namely the re-establishing of Republican–Socialist coalition government.[11] In this the PCE entirely concurred, equally preferring a Republican–Socialist coalition, or even an entirely republican government, as would become clear later from their initial reluctance over accepting Largo Caballero's designation of two PCE ministers in September 1936.[12]

At the beginning of May 1936, however, against a background of heightened domestic tension as the Right, as a consequence of the February *débâcle*, took the fight against reform beyond the parliamentary arena, Prieto's attempt to strengthen the Popular Front against an increasingly likely military reaction was effectively checked by the party Left. The Caballeristas stood absolutely opposed to Prieto in his bid to take over as prime minister. The mechanics of that obstruction belong to the detailed history of the party dispute. Suffice it to say here that among the reformist socialists who controlled the party executive, Prieto was considered to have made a grave tactical error even to have consulted the Left.[13] Azaña, as the newly elected President, had not made Prieto's acceptance conditional on the unanimous support of his party and the socialist executive itself urged him to accept the premiership regardless, in that he would not be breaking party discipline and, even more importantly, because, in the event, Largo Caballero, the leader of the left wing, would not use his control of the socialist minority against Prieto in the Cortes.[14] However, in that Prieto chose to decline the power being offered to the socialists without even having recourse to the full range of inner-party mechanisms to bolster his case, he appears to have lacked the courage of his convictions as a statesman, as had been exhibited in abundance in his Cuenca speech. This being the case, then he must himself bear part of the responsibility for the fatal undermining of the republican government in the spring of 1936.[15]

Indalecio Prieto's attempt to secure the premiership in May had been the complement of a two-part strategy whose first principle had been the elevation of Azaña to the presidency at the beginning of May. To remove the strong man of progressive republicanism, and the single most important factor of cohesion between the parties of the Left, at a moment of such enormous political tension could only be justified if he could definitely be substituted by someone whose political capacity was equal both to the previous premier's and to the needs of a situation in which the acute threat of military reaction loomed increasingly large. That such a gap could only be filled by Prieto was well appreciated by everyone. However, it was equally well known that the party Left was absolutely opposed to further socialist collaboration in government and had threatened to break up the Popular Front should such a scenario be realised. The hostility of the Left did not suddenly spring forth when Prieto put forward his proposal and one must therefore reassess the soundness of Prieto's political judgement. If he was not certain of being able to convince the Left to allow him to lead a coalition and, equally, he was not prepared either to forge ahead regardless or to manoeuvre within the party to the certain detriment of an already fragile unity, then, clearly, he should not have supported Azaña's promotion with all the force of his vital and dynamic personality. Casares Quiroga as prime minister in the 'hot' summer of 1936 was far too high a price to pay for the luxury of toppling the former president, Alcalá Zamora. Nor can the Left be held responsible for a shortcoming which was fundamentally Prieto's. The Caballeristas had long held to their policy of obstructing every initiative to resurrect the Republican–Socialist coalition government. In that this was so, the responsibility was Prieto's to break or circumvent the political obstacle they posed, rather than the Caballeristas' to abandon that policy. The weight of political responsibility borne by the party Left was considerable but it consisted not in the fact that it wrecked Prieto's coalition option, but that, in having achieved as much, it failed to substitute any alternative policy.[16]

In the period between Casares Quiroga's assumption of the premiership in May and the military coup in July, relations between the reformists in the PSOE and the Left, with its stronghold in the Madrid Socialist group and the national executive of the UGT, became strained to breaking point. The break finally came at the beginning of July when the UGT executive, and therefore the socialist Left, rejected the party executive's proposal for a joint committee of all the organisations comprising the Popular Front with the object of coordinating defensive action against the impending military reaction.[17] As a justification of its veto, the union leadership adduced the party executive's own rejection previously of a similar proposal it had made in conjunction with the PCE in March 1936.[18] The military coup thus caught the one party able to give powerful support to the Popular Front strategy in Spain, divided in a vitriolic internal dispute that diverted its energies and incapacitated it as a force to be used to forestall and defuse the catastrophism of the Right.

While Prieto, as the driving force of the party executive at that point, had rejected the initial joint committee proposal in March partly because of his conviction that the Popular Front strategy was primarily a parliamentary one, there was at least an element of suspicion of the Left and all its works. Equally, the socialist Left was intensely suspicious of Prieto's constant warnings of an impending military coup. The Caballeristas interpreted this as yet another of Prieto's ploys to bring about socialist re-entry into government. However, it was also true that in order to sustain a minimally logical basis for the passivity which constituted their only policy, the socialist Left had perforce to underplay the threat of a military coup.[19] Indeed between October 1934 and 1936, Luis Araquistain, as spokesman for the Left, proclaimed on more than one occasion that military *pronunciamientos* no longer had a realistic chance of success and that the spirit prevailing among the military was one of reform.[20] To give the socialist Left the benefit of the doubt, the publicising of such views could be interpreted as an attempt to influence the military opinion of which Araquistain spoke, and thus to bring about just such a spirit of reform. However, Araquistain's contention, that those officers who inclined towards a military coup would effectively be neutralised by their own soldiers, was, to say the least, open to dispute. It ignored the experience of October 1934 when the problem of the potentially dubious loyalty of Spanish conscripts had been circumvented by the use of both the Army of Africa and the Foreign Legion.

Just as, internationally, neither the syndical nor the intellectual wing of the socialist Left considered that Nazism posed a serious threat – because fascism was seen as being effectively one step nearer socialism, and in the final confrontation the victory of the latter was assured – likewise, in the domestic arena, the basis of Caballerista non-action was equally determinist. It was claimed that any attempt to impose a military dictatorship was extremely unlikely, but should such an attempt be made, then a preventative, spontaneous popular revolution would immediately occur. Characteristically, of course, the accent was on spontaneity; the concept of revolution remained an abstract one. No blueprint for the revolutionary seizure of power was elaborated, nor was any preparation of the socialist base undertaken.[21] Indeed, it is curious that in their eagerness to counter Prieto's warnings, both the party Left and Casares Quiroga resorted to the same formula response: that the military should make its bid for power and then its rebellion could be definitively broken.[22]

While it would be unfair to lay the entire responsibility for the failure of the Popular Front initiative to confront and defuse the military threat at the door of the PSOE, it is important to recognise that the deadlock within the party had a profoundly destabilising effect which no other political group was able to counter, at least before 18 July. It is true that discipline in the socialist minority was by and large maintained. Largo's supporters voted with the Prietistas and refrained from tabling awkward questions about the origins of street violence and the destabilising tactics of the Right.[23] This undoubtedly contributed to the immediate stability of the precarious republican government, but such measures were inevitably piecemeal and they calmed the symptoms without ever attacking the cause of the malady.

The reality was that neither Casares Quiroga nor any member of the cabinet he had chosen was capable of even appreciating the gravity of the situation facing the Republic by the summer of 1936, much less resolving it. Casares' own repeated and frenzied denials of the validity of the socialist leader's extremely reliable reports of military conspiracy are now notorious.[24] Whether Casares believed his own pronouncements must remain a matter for conjecture. However, what is certain is that there were those in the ranks of conservative and even moderate republicanism who, faced with the evidence of the tremendous political polarisation which had occurred between 1934 and 1936, were no longer convinced that the greatest threat to the Republic, such as they conceived it, came from the military conspirators. A majority within the republican groupings harboured an immense fear of the extent of the aspirations of the social base of Popular Front which they saw as verging on social and economic revolution. The southern land occupations were viewed with rising panic. In order to appreciate the real origins of the passivity of the republican government in the spring and summer of 1936, which developed into a total paralysis of the institutions of state after the military coup, it is necessary to appreciate that the republican parties, always a fragile minority, felt themselves to be trapped between the two extremes of military reaction and *de facto* popular revolution, and the Republican majority by no means believed the former to be the greater danger.

THE POPULAR REVOLUTION VERSUS THE POPULAR FRONT

It has been well documented that the military rising of 17 and 18 July 1936 unleashed a spontaneous grass-roots revolution throughout the area which was held for the Republic. The massive popular collectivisation of industry and agriculture was the vital practical concomitant of the popular defence of a Republic whose power structure was all but totally paralysed, just as it was also the fulfilment of the thoroughgoing social and economic reform, long aspired to, which provided the motive force for the revolutionary defence of a bourgeois Republic.[25]

This popular revolution which the left socialist leader, Francisco Largo Caballero, was called upon initially to pacify, and thereafter to subdue and dominate with the institutions of state, was in essence the temporary victory of the social base of the Popular Front electoral pact over both the moderate reformist programme of the Republican–Socialist coalition and the new Comintern line of Popular Front in Europe. In France Thorez had said that the Popular Front was not the revolution; as a strategy of government nor was it, of course, in Spain.[26]

However, for a time during the months of the popular revolutionary defence of the Second Republic, it seemed as if the Popular Front was the dynamic of the revolution. In many areas of loyalist Spain, Popular Front committees were appearing at both the local and provincial level, functioning as organs of parallel power whilst those of the state, *ayuntamientos* and *diputaciones*, town halls and county councils respectively, remained in eclipse.[27] In the early stages of the war these Popular Front committees were as uneven in their constitution as they were in geographical distribution. However, in general, both the constitution and the name of these local and provincial committees depended on the relative strength of the political forces in a given area. Where the CNT, or the CNT and the UGT, were most powerful, then the committees of parallel power would often be called committees of syndical unity. The very fact that in certain localities the committees bore the name Popular Front suggests the predominance of political parties over unions and specifically over the CNT.

The grass-roots revolution in the loyalist zone effectively made the left socialists the titular masters of the political scene. It was by no means the case that the Caballeristas had been any closer to the source of the revolution than any other leadership group on the Left, nor did the socialist Left leadership attempt to harness its force. The revolution, in that it was a rank-and-file phenomenon, temporarily eclipsed the national leaderships of all parties and organisations. However, the revolutionary image of the left socialists – although it was soon to be revealed as pure rhetoric covering an inveterately reformist practice, as the Prietistas had always judged it to be – was sufficient to bring it the task of forming what would be the first Spanish government which reflected the constitution of the electoral pact of February 1936. Largo Caballero, veteran socialist and General Secretary of the UGT, was appointed as prime minister on 4 September, thereby eclipsing, temporarily at least, the party reformists and Indalecio Prieto, particularly, who had been serving as chief adviser to Giral's republican administration in the months since its appointment on 20 July. During this period both the socialist party executive and Prieto had envisaged themselves as on the brink of claiming the government and premiership which had been lost in May. The realisation that popular revolution precluded such a possibility came as a considerable blow.[28] Throughout July and August Prieto had, by throwing himself into a frenzy of activity as Giral's right-hand man, managed to avoid acknowledging the fact that a moderate Republican–Socialist coalition, as he had always envisaged Popular Front, was out of the question and that any strengthening of the executive power of the Republic would be bound to give the advantage to Largo and governmental form to the 'entelechy' of the electoral pact.[29] In the end it was the effective withdrawal of the Giral government which forced the issue on Azaña. Largo, with a keen awareness of the strength of his position, refused any compromise formula of an enlarged government including representatives of both wings of the PSOE over which Giral would continue to preside, and in such circumstances Prieto and the socialist executive were forced to accept the inevitable.[30]

The fact that the socialist Left had assumed control of the central political power, apart from the implications for the dispute in the party, apparently signified the victory of the popular revolution, and thereby of the radical aspirations of the social base of February 1936, over the moderate programme of government reform. Indeed, the reformist socialist Juan Negrín, future prime minister of the Spanish Popular Front and finance minister in Largo Caballero's cabinets, criticised the latter's appointment as the victory of October 1934. Equally, it was this view which prompted the misgivings of the Spanish republicans and the Comintern over Largo's appointment as prime minister; after the *volte-face* of the Seventh Congress the Comintern's desire to contain popular revolution was indistinguishable from the republicans' fear of it.[31] However, both Azaña and Prieto appreciated the impossibility of governing democratically entirely against the popular will. Prieto was convinced of the reformist reality underlying the Left's veneer of revolutionary rhetoric and came, albeit reluctantly and with a sense of deep personal disappointment, to accept that, given the domestic political conjuncture, Largo was the only possible choice as prime minister. Indeed, he even came to appreciate that Largo would be fulfilling a crucial function first in pacifying and subsequently in controlling and containing the forces of popular revolution; and in fact, that it was a task which, ironically, the socialist Left was uniquely equipped to undertake.

The only disadvantage, but it was a significant one, concerned the international dimension of the war. The reformist socialists, the Comintern and the republicans shared a concept of the war which singled out the sphere of international relations as the vital factor of victory.[32] For the socialists and their Popular Front allies it was imperative that the domestic policies of the Republic should be geared to winning the support of the Western democracies. However, just as domestically the Spanish oligarchy, and even considerable sections of the middle class, had accepted the revolutionary rhetoric of the socialist Left at face value, so the fear was that international perceptions of the

Spanish Republic as 'red' or revolutionary would deprive it of the material support which, given that Germany and Italy had already been seen to line up with the insurgent forces, would be absolutely vital to its victory. However, for a time, in fact up to May 1937, the requirements of domestic politics were to take priority over those of foreign policy – although this is a false division where the republican war effort is concerned. The fundamental objective of that domestic policy itself was the creation of a war effort which would be suitable for export as propaganda, designed to secure the intervention of Britain and France and the lifting of the embargo on the sale of arms to the Republic.[33]

The isolation of Britain and France had been identified very early on, from the stage of proto non-intervention as it might be termed, as potentially the greatest source of damage to the loyalist war effort. This forecast proved to be correct not only in the most obvious way – in that shortages of war *matériel* inevitably resulted – but also because the distortion of the balance of political power attendant on the Republic's reliance on the Soviet Union as its sole major supplier inevitably had a disastrous effect on political unity in the republican zone.

During the war the PSOE itself experienced enormous frustration at the crisis of the international socialist movement – both its political and labour wings – when confronted with the conflict in Spain. The contribution of International Socialism consisted in numerous declarations of moral solidarity and little else. By comparison, it was manifestly obvious that the organisations of the Third International were providing support of quite a different order. This, inevitably, did nothing to enhance either the prestige or the authority of the Spanish Socialist Party. If, in public, the PSOE never ceased alternating moderate, reasoned argument with impassioned plea – how the defence of the Spanish Republic should be seen by the Western democracies as no more than an act of basic self-defence against international fascist aggression – in the relative privacy of national and executive committee meetings the anger and bitterness at what was perceived as an attitude of political and moral betrayal were made very plain.[34] Even publicly, Indalecio Prieto declared that it was hard for the PSOE to appear as either credible or authoritative or even remotely dynamic, as compared to the PCE, when the International to which the PSOE belonged was doing nothing for the Spanish Republic.[35] In contrast, the PCE was very obviously benefiting in terms of an expanding membership and increasing political influence as a result of Soviet and Third International support for the republican cause.

The socialist movements in France and Britain were respectively frightened and divided, and frightened and the obedient followers of government policy. In the case of Britain, in September 1936 the TUC Congress had approved the policy of non-intervention by 3 029 000 votes to 51 000. This was followed by the Labour Party's endorsement of the policy at its Edinburgh conference in October of the same year.[36] However, the conflict of political interest and principles over Spain was particularly acute in the French Socialist Party, the SFIO. That there existed a clear ideological affinity between the French and Spanish governments is undeniable but, in the last analysis, the precarious position of the French Popular Front domestically, with the considerable forces of the French establishment ranged against it, meant that the hands of the socialist prime minister, Léon Blum, were effectively tied. The overwhelming fear in France was that intervention in favour of the Spanish Republic would mean exposure to German aggression and, furthermore, exposure in isolation, as Britain had made it clear that should intervention in the Spanish war be the cause of a German attack on French territory, then she would consider herself absolved from her defence obligations to France. This attitude of the British government, which crystallised logically in non-intervention, effectively crippled the French Popular Front as far as providing aid for the Republic was concerned. In both Britain and France the tremendous weight of pacifism in the European labour movement, which was the legacy of the First World War, also worked to the detriment of the socialist cause in Spain. So it was in this context of the paralysis and passivity of the International Socialist movement that Spanish socialism had to compete with the PCE and confront the massive practical problems on the home front.[37]

Loyalist acceptance of the political influence of the Soviet Union, exerted via its diplomatic representatives in Spain and the Comintern, stemmed from the early realisation in Spanish circles that the material support of the Soviet Union would be vital to the survival of the Republic. Largo Caballero's personal adviser, Luis Araquistain, was convinced that Soviet aid would become crucial; his experience of the political and diplomatic climate in Paris in the early months of the war while attempting to negotiate supplies of war *matériel* for the Republic, had convinced him that the French government would be certain to default on aid.[38] This had immediate implications for the domestic politics of the Popular Front in Spain for, such was his conviction, he persuaded an extremely reluctant Largo to accept the ardent fellow-travelling socialist, Alvarez del Vayo, as Foreign Minister in his cabinet of September 1936. It had fully been the intention that Araquistain himself would serve as Minister of Foreign Affairs and his name had been included in the list which the prime minister designate had presented to Azaña. It was the President himself who pointed out that pressure had been brought to bear and that the Soviet choice was Alvarez del Vayo. Araquistain argued that a compromise solution would be worthwhile and that it would be possible to control Alvarez del Vayo by a judicious choice of ministry staff. Although this sufficed to convince Largo, who accepted the premiership of a modified cabinet, what the Caballeristas underestimated was the difficulty not only of controlling their Foreign Minister but also of containing or limiting Soviet interference in both the political and military spheres. Such a containment would become virtually impossible precisely because of the increasing isolation of the Republic as a result of non-intervention.[39]

The constitution of the two national governments headed by Largo clearly reflected the reality of a radically altered power base in republican Spain, albeit that this would prove a temporary phenomenon. The determination of the left socialist leader to bind all significant political forces in the loyalist zone to government responsibility was a means of reducing the risk of damaging criticism being made from the freedom of opposition, just as it was also the realisation of Largo's ideal of working-class unity, conceived, as always, as unity under the tutelage of the historic party of Pablo Iglesias. However, on examination, both the constitution of Largo's governments and the manner of their formation reveal their weakness in disparity and, specifically, the incoherence at their centre consequent upon the division in the PSOE. The very manner of Largo's acceptance of the government mandate itself served to aggravate the bitterness of the party divide. For, in contrast to Prieto in May, with his punctilious respect for party discipline and also, most probably, his fear of opposition from the Left in the Cortes, Largo in September did not even seek to obtain ratification of his appointment from the socialist executive, thus contravening both the spirit and the letter of party discipline.[40] The socialist executive was requested to suggest individuals to fill its requisite number of ministerial posts, as were the other political parties and organisations, but it was not asked to underwrite Largo's acceptance of the premiership.

From the very beginning in September 1936 Largo Caballero had sought to persuade the CNT to join his government, the anarchist trade union being the greatest potential source of criticism and therefore the greatest threat to his authority. However, with a high-handedness characteristic of the socialist Left's dealings with other working-class organisations, initially Largo was only prepared to offer the CNT a single post, and that without portfolio, in spite of the fact that participation in government required an enormous compromise of fundamental ideological principle on the part of the anarchist organisation. Although the principle of participation in government was accepted, thus initiating the massive crisis within the movement, the rejection of Largo's initial offer as beneath the dignity of the CNT resulted in the exclusion of the anarchists from central government until the formation of Largo's second cabinet at the beginning of November.[41]

The modification of the national government and the final acceptance by the anarchists of four ministries – Justice, Public Health, and Trade and Industry which was split into two separate portfolios – in effect signified a defeat for the principle of apoliticism and for the more radical tendency within the CNT, which had been arguing for a complete reorganisation of the politico-juridical structure of the state in order to reflect the dramatic alteration in the balance of social and economic power, specifically in the relations of production, which had taken place as a consequence of the military rising.[42] Largo Caballero opposed every attempt by the CNT to negotiate any alteration in the structure of the Popular Front and especially the proposal of a National Defence Committee on which the two trade unions would have had a majority representation, thus highlighting the essential reformism of the socialist Left. Ideologically it belonged not with the anarchists, but with those opposing any transformation of the state apparatus. Largo, by overseeing the reconstruction of the central state power and defending the reformist order of the Popular Front as it had existed prior to 18 July 1936, effectively achieved the containment of the forces of popular revolution which, although vanguardless, had posed a threat to that order. The achievement, however, was to cost the socialist Left dear. The exercise of political power in the supremely difficult initial phase of the war created enormous stresses which the socialist Left was ill equipped to absorb. The experience of government merely accelerated the process of disintegration until by May 1937 the socialist Left was an entirely spent force.[43]

In November 1936 it was Largo who had forced Azaña to sanction the inclusion of the four anarchist ministers, threatening his own resignation if the President failed to overcome his strong personal reservations. Clearly, for Azaña and the republicans, the entry of anarchists into the government was not only politically distasteful from a purely personal perspective, it was also considered as seriously undermining the image of the Republic internationally, thus further reducing the already remote possibility of securing aid from France or Britain.[44] Likewise for the PCE, the presence of anarchists in the republican government ran contrary to the Soviet objective of collective security against international fascist aggression, and for identical reasons. Indeed, such was the concern over the international image of the Republic that even the inclusion of the two PCE representatives in Largo's cabinets was only conceded when the latter had insisted upon it as the pre-condition of his accepting the premiership.

The government which emerged from the reorganisation at the beginning of November was part of Largo's attempt to unify the political and military aims of the loyalist war effort by amalgamating all the political forces hostile to the insurgents in his national government of the Popular Front. Yet the mere accumulation of representatives could not remove the essential contradiction or incompatibility between reformist and revolutionary politico-military strategies for fighting the civil war, and the inclusion of the anarchist ministers signified nothing more than the crisis of acratic theory as reflected in the internal division of the organisation.

The bitter conflict over political principles fought out with such violence behind the republican lines – the primacy of revolution versus the primacy of war, as it is usually expressed – was in essence a conflict over the objectives of the war.[45] Whether the loyalists opted for a revolutionary war effort, extensively employing guerrilla tactics, extending the process of industrial and agricultural collectivisation and fomenting rebellion in Spanish Morocco to cut the nationalists off from the source of their best troops; or whether they opted for a conventional war effort, as means radically change ends, so the choice would determine absolutely the nature of post-war society. In reality, however, once Largo Caballero had assumed control of the republican government and had begun to reassert the authority of the state, the notion of a choice no longer existed except as a theoretical abstraction. The left socialist leadership and the prime minister himself were squarely ranged with the republicans, the communists and the reformist socialists in sustaining the primacy of Popular Front reformism, and therefore of a conventional war effort.

Undoubtedly the prime minister's innate pragmatism had been substantially reinforced by the series of grave militia defeats in the south during August 1936 and, most specifically, by the bloody massacre at Badajoz in the middle of the month. The pressing need to halt the rebel advance made the militarisation of the militia and the building of a regular, hierarchical army, if a 'popular' one, almost inevitable. However, Largo's policy options were, across the board, those of the reformist socialists.[46] Just as the basis of his foreign policy – the reliance on convincing the French, and therefore the British government, actively to support the Republic – attested to his desire to reconstruct and maintain the bourgeois democratic structure of the Republic, like any reformist socialist, so too did his determination to rebuild the central state power, to nationalise and centralise the control of industry, and to limit the extent of collectivisation by decree.

Largo's correspondence, likewise, all attests to his reformism and his defence of the Popular Front option. In his letter to Ben Tillett, in August 1936, he emphasised that the socialists were fighting for the victory of democracy but that it was not their objective to establish a socialist society; and in an interview with the journalist Charles Reichmann, he insisted that the constitution of a purely socialist government had never been the order of the day.[47] However, most significant in the Spanish context was the exchange of letters with the veteran anarchist, Federico Urales, in February 1937.[48] The essential condition of victory, Largo stressed, was discipline on both the military and civilian fronts. The only command which had to be obeyed was that of the national government. Like Negrín after him, Largo was also striving to achieve for the central government supreme control of political, military and economic affairs throughout the republican zone and, also like Negrín, he was prepared to confront opposition from the regions in the pursuit of this objective.[49] On 1 February 1937, in his speech to the Cortes, Largo emphatically set his face against anarchist experiments – '*ya se ha ensayado bastante*', enough of revolutionary experimentation. For, unlike the FNTT – the Socialist Landworkers' Federation which supported him and which during the period of the Second Republic had constituted the militant nucleus of *caballerismo* as a phenomenon of mass radicalisation – Largo never seriously took issue with the communist Minister of Agriculture, Vicente Uribe, over his policy which was far from favourable to the collectives, whether they were anarchist or socialist.[50]

The government of November 1936 was a massive and unwieldy affair totalling eighteen ministers, including Largo himself who held both the premiership and the war portfolio. If such a formation was to operate with even a minimum of cohesion and efficiency, it needed a dynamic and coherent nucleus which would function as an organising principle. As in the period of the Second Republic, this ought to have been provided by the PSOE. However, not only was there the ever-deepening divide between the two wings of the party, a legacy of the republican period, but, as a result of the cumulative political and military tensions of the war, there also occurred a further fragmentation. This arose because of the deteriorating state of relations between the left socialist representatives in the cabinet and the wing of the party with which they were increasingly only nominally associated.[51]

The Caballeristas lacked any policy initiative which could properly be called their own, much less a revolutionary blueprint, and they thus proceeded merely to implement the basis of Prieto's reformist programme, setting themselves up as the maximum defenders of Popular Front – a policy option which they had seen fit to block in May 1936. It is thus understandable, at the subjective level, that the socialist executive and the ministers appointed by it should have maintained a certain distance from the left socialists in government, whom they considered not only guilty of political hypocrisy but also, much more seriously, responsible for the enforced socialist passivity of the crucial months before the military coup. However, the net result was a weakening of the party's position as a whole.

Although the erosion of the PSOE as a mass party stretches far beyond its disintegration at the level of government, it was that fragmentation which was mainly responsible for the eclipse of the socialist leadership while an increasingly dynamic PCE, having once provided the originality which helped enormously in capturing mass support for the Popular Front option, grew to fill the vacuum of support for the Front in wartime – the result of the chronic political paralysis of Spanish republicanism and the division in the PSOE.[52] In the war years the PCE assumed many of the functions that an undivided PSOE, given its historical trajectory, would have assumed in other circumstances. While it is true that the PCE was something of a hybrid party during the civil war in terms of the class basis of its membership, and also that a great deal of its political influence in the period stemmed from the fact that it was the channel by which vital Soviet aid reached the beleaguered Republic, it would be a distortion to see the emergence of the party as the mainstay of Popular Front during the war as the result of subtle machinations by which the PSOE was destroyed and the Republic subverted in the interests of Soviet foreign policy. The received wisdom, such as it is, has most definitely been refracted through a Cold War prism and historical accuracy has suffered badly as a result. The energy and dynamism of the PCE have been expanded to the dimensions of myth. That the party was possessed of a great organisational ability is undoubtedly true, such is almost the defining characteristic of communist parties. But its dynamism was, in the last analysis, a relative phenomenon; relative, that is, to the debility and division of the other political forces in the loyalist zone.[53]

Indalecio Prieto, as the politician who epitomised the reformist experiment of Popular Front in Spain, fell into the trap of which he himself had warned the party Left.[54] For, in adopting during the first year of the war a tactic which fundamentally consisted of waiting upon the political exhaustion of the socialist Left, Prieto had apparently forgotten his own words of caution at Egea de los Caballeros in May 1936 when he emphasised that the erosion of any one element of the Popular Front would inevitably damage the stability of the Front as a whole.

The crisis of Largo's government was latent both in the cabinet and in the street by the beginning of February 1937. On 14 February, just after the fall of Malaga, a demonstration organised by the provincial secretariat of the UGT in Valencia, in support of Largo, was effectively neutralised by a PCE-inspired swamping action which shifted the emphasis to that of a general display of support for the government's war effort.[55] The disintegration of any left socialist identity in the cabinet meant Largo's increased isolation, and the hostility of republicans, moderate socialists and communists was hardening rapidly into a resolve to act. Largo's appointment as prime minister had been a necessity in a period of revolutionary turmoil and state disintegration. However, now that Largo had successfully achieved the common objective – the containment of the revolutionary threat – his continued control of the cabinet was seen as an anachronism, and an unaffordable one at that, given the logic of the Republic's foreign policy. In addition, the exercise of power had exposed the vulnerability of the socialist Left in that it had revealed both the incoherence of its power base and the ideological bankruptcy of its trade union leadership.

It is in such a context that both the May 1937 cabinet crisis, culminating in the fall of Largo Caballero, and the revolutionary explosion in Barcelona, the famous 'May Days', which preceded it, need to be understood – as the liquidation of the vestiges of revolutionary power by the political representatives of the central state. In May 1937 Largo Caballero was destroyed, not by the voracity or cunning of the PCE, but rather by the inexorable logic of a process of revolutionary containment, effectively counter-revolution, which he himself had set in motion. Largo had performed a crucial task in the supremely difficult initial phase of the war. He had salvaged the structure of the bourgeois Republic and it was this, significantly strengthened, which swept him away.[56]

Both the communists and the socialists, however, had other motives for attacking the socialist Left. Whilst at one level the communist leadership could never view Largo's premiership in a favourable light because its symbolic significance ran absolutely contrary to the PCE's commitment to the Popular Front and thus to the achieving of inter-class alliances both nationally and internationally; at another level popular frontism, considered in its entirety as both a parliamentary and an extra-parliamentary strategy, in Spain as elsewhere, was a policy which theoretically gave communist parties the opportunity to compete on an equal basis with other well established working-class parties and organisations which were numerically much stronger. The complementary structure of *frente único* at grass-roots level – that is, unity from below, cutting across organisational divisions in order to strengthen unity from above via the Popular Front – meant that communist parties, with, almost by definition, a high level of organisational ability, potentially had the means of reversing the usual balance of political power as based on numerical strength and parliamentary and union influence – criteria which tended to favour socialist organisations.[57]

Indeed, in the Spanish case, with military reaction, revolution and civil war, so extreme was the situation created that the PCE saw its chance to press immediately beyond *frente único* to its ultimate logical conclusion: the amalgamation of the Spanish Socialist and Communist Parties in a single class party, the *partido único*. Given the existence in Spain in 1936 of what was termed the 'climate of unity', that is, the overwhelming popular desire to break down the organisational barriers between the various working-class forces in the belief that working-class unity was equal to working-class strength, it was felt both by the representatives of the Comintern in Spain and the leaders of the PCE that the argument in favour of socialist–communist unity was an irresistible one which could not but carry all before it – not least the bureaucratic preoccupations, organisational jealousies and suspicions of the socialist leadership. However, the Comintern and the PCE had omitted a vital factor from their calculations. They had reckoned without the obstinacy of Largo himself, for whom the effective loss of the radicalised Socialist Youth to a Stalinist PCE in April 1936 had served as a salutary lesson. Thereafter, the wily trade union leader was to the fore. Throughout the second half of 1936 and the early months of 1937, considerable and increasing pressure was exerted upon Largo to bring about the unification of the Socialist and Communist Parties via the good offices of both the Comintern representative, Medina (Víctor Codovila), and the Soviet ambassador, Marcel Rosenberg. This, however, was to no avail. Neither Stalin's letters, nor his personal entreaty that the class parties be unified, served to move the Spanish prime minister.[58] It was this constant pressure over party unification which was responsible for the notorious ejection of the Soviet ambassador from the prime minister's office.[59] Thus it was Largo's intransigence over party unity, together with his refusal to sanction, after the May events in Barcelona, an extension of the Soviet purges to Spanish republican territory in the shape of a Stalinist witch-hunt against the dissident communist POUM, which added a sectarian motive to the PCE's more general political disapproval, thereby increasing its determination to remove Largo from power.

Nevertheless, in order fully to appreciate the fundamental causes of the cabinet crisis of May 1937 and the suddenness of the Caballerista collapse, they need to be seen as the inevitable result of the failure of the left socialists to consolidate an alternative power base on the left which could have provided them with the support needed to survive the collective onslaught of the PCE and the reformists in their own party. However, Largo had overseen the restoration of central state power and had thus been the architect of counter-revolution, and this naturally inhibited the rapprochement between the socialist Left and the anarchist organisation which might have saved it in May 1937.

For the PSOE executive and all those who had aligned themselves with it, Largo's forced resignation was seen as a victory for party legitimacy and an opportunity to repair the damage to party discipline inflicted by a rogue Left for more than a year.[60] The withdrawal of the socialist Left from government marked the beginning of a determined purge against Caballeristas in the party and union organisation. The ultimate consequence of this was a legacy of bitterness so extreme that it poisoned successive decades of exile until the emergence of a new, assertive, post-war generation of Spanish socialists in the interior who had no direct experience of the bitter divisions of the 1930s. The immediate consequence, however, was a widening division in the ranks of the socialist organisation which further undermined the stability of the republican government just as, ironically, Juan Negrín's appointment as prime minister in May restored the original project of a Popular Front in Spain. The government he constituted was, in its overall structure, as near to the shape of Republican–Socialist reformist coalition as the new conjuncture of wartime political forces would permit. The ministerial portfolios were almost tactical appointments, as Negrín himself admitted.[61] If under-secretaries are taken into account then the links between the Popular Front government and the PSOE were stronger and closer under Negrín than was ever the case before.[62] Equally, the constitution of the Negrín government meant that those with considerable experience of international politics, and who saw that dimension as the crucial factor in a republican victory, had a virtual monopoly of political power in Spain.[63]

The progressive erosion of the Popular Front and the political fragmentation and disintegration of its component parts meant that, of necessity, the PCE became increasingly important to Negrín, who, whatever his political shortcomings, had a breadth of vision which enabled him to see that the notion of a negotiated peace or a political compromise with Franco was a dangerous chimera.[64] While a detailed analysis of the process of erosion lies beyond the scope of this chapter, it is clear that if one attempts to define the nature of the much-quoted but suspiciously vague 'disillusion' at the apparent communist hegemony in the republican zone by late 1938, then one is really analysing the progressive disintegration of the Popular Front pact as an inter-class alliance.

Effectively, the Popular Front broke down because of the convergence of two different sorts of war weariness. Firstly, there was a very general and widely felt exhaustion among the Spanish proletariat, the result of nearly thirty months of a civil war which had brought only cumulative material deprivation at home and a sense of growing despair in the face of an ever-bleaker international situation. This reached its nadir at Munich in September 1938, when not only Czechoslovakia but also the Spanish Republic was sacrificed on the altar of appeasement. But even more far reaching in its effects was the demoralisation of the middle classes, and specifically the perspective of financial and industrial interests in Catalonia – the very groups which constituted the power base of the PCE. For these groups the PCE was no longer a saviour, it was no longer seen either as providing protection against revolution and disorder or as a vehicle for winning the war; rather it had become the abiding obstacle to a negotiated settlement with Franco and the oligarchic interests which he represented. In Catalonia, the interests of capital naturally stood opposed to the principle of a scorched earth tactic because it would necessarily have entailed the destruction of factories, workshops and the capital equipment therein.

It was thus in the face of working-class exhaustion and a vacillating and discontented middle class that the PCE found itself increasingly isolated and, for the first time, unable to mobilise any class behind a rapidly disintegrating Popular Front. The Casado coup, which effectively put an end to republican resistance, was much more than just a rebellion of the republican military. It signified the convergence of diametrically opposed political and social interests against a Communist Party which, while it had alienated anarchists and some socialists by its protagonism in the destruction of popular revolution in the interests of Popular Front, had equally alienated its middle-class power base by 'failing' to deliver the military victory on which the political commitment of the bourgeoisie had ultimately always depended.

Notes

1. The signatories were as follows: PSOE, UGT, PCE, POUM, Izquierda Republicana (Azaña), Unión Republicana (Martínez Barrio), the Catalan Esquerra and the Partido Sindicalista (Angel Pestaña).
2. M. Bizcarrondo, *Araquistain y la Crisis Socialista en la II República/ Leviatán 1934–1936* (Madrid, 1975) p. 348.
3. For the origins of the Popular Front in Spain see, Santos Juliá, *Orígenes del Frente Popular en España: 1934–1936* (Madrid, 1979). For the communists' change of tactic see, Bizcarrondo, *Araquistain y la Crisis Socialista*, pp. 346–59 and Juliá, *Orígenes del Frente Popular*, pp. 83–93.
4. Prieto's speech at Torrelodones 9 August 1933, 'El Liberal de Bilbao' reprinted in E. Malefakis (ed.), *Discursos Fundamentales* (Madrid, 1975) p. 170.
5. Ibid., p. 255, speech at Cuenca 1 May 1936, 'La Conquista Interior de España'.
6. Paul Preston, *The Coming of the Spanish Civil War* (London, 1978).
7. Juliá, *Orígenes del Frente Popular*, p. 106; M. Bizcarrondo, 'Desde las alianzas obreras al Frente Popular', in *Estudios de Historia Social*, no. 16–17, January–June 1981, p. 103.
8. S. Juliá, *La Izquierda del PSOE (1935–1936)* (Madrid, 1977) p. 231.
9. Bizcarrondo, 'Desde las alianzas obreras', p. 100.
10. Juliá, *Orígenes del Frente Popular*, p. 105.
11. Prieto's comment in May 1936, referring to the Popular Front pact was: 'That was before the elections, but now this business of a Popular Front ought already to have been laid to rest, in fact without it ever really having existed at all'; in J. S. Vidarte, *Todos Fuimos Culpables*, volume 1 (Barcelona, 1977) p. 99.
12. Burnett Bolloten, *The Spanish Revolution: The Left and the Struggle for Power during the Civil War* (Chapel Hill, 1979) p. 122.
13. Vidarte, *Todos Fuimos Culpables*, pp. 119–22; Preston, *The Coming of the Spanish Civil War*, p. 192.
14. Ibid. For Azaña's position see, Vidarte, *Todos Fuimos Culpables*, p. 664.
15. For a defence/explanation of Prieto's hesitancy see, L. Romero Solano, *Vísperas de la Guerra de España* (Mexico, 1947) pp. 160–1.
16. Juliá, *La Izquierda del PSOE*, p. 109.

17. Minutes of the UGT executive, 6 March 1936, Fundación Pablo Iglesias, Madrid; Bizcarrondo, 'Desde las alianzas obreras', p. 104.
18. For Prieto's veto see, Vidarte, *Todos Fuimos Culpables*, p. 95; UGT minutes, 29 March 1936.
19. For a detailed study of left socialist 'theory', international fascism and the military threat in Spain see, Juliá, *La Izquierda del PSOE*, pp. 265–86.
20. Ibid., p. 256, quoting Araquistain: 'In their heart of hearts, the officers are not really soldiers, they're bureaucrats. There are always vague rumours that a coup is being planned, but nothing ever happens. What the army does constitute is a *potential* danger.'
21. M. Tuñón de Lara in F. Torres (ed.), *Teoría y Práctica del Movimiento Obrero en España (1900–1936)* (Valencia, 1977) p. 52: 'Lacking any theoretical basis, Caballero confused his own state of mind with the social structure and conjunction of Spain in the 1930s. He went on to propose the strategy of a workers' front by means of which there would be launched a head-on attack against the political and economic establishment, with the object of making a full proletarian revolution. Yet not once did he consider who might serve as his allies nor which social forces would have to be neutralised.'
22. Juliá, *Izquierda del PSOE*, p. 279.
23. Preston, *The Coming of the Spanish Civil War*, p. 197.
24. Ibid., p. 193; Vidarte, *Todos Fuimos Culpables*, pp. 146–7, 190–1.
25. M. Tuñón de Lara, *Estudios de Historia Social*, no. 16–17, January–June 1981, p. 127.
26. Compare the remark of José Díaz, General Secretary of the PCE, in a speech on 1 June 1936, 'before resorting to strike action, all other strategies must first have been exhausted', with the famous one of Maurice Thorez, leader of the French Communist Party, that it was not only necessary to know how to begin a strike, but also how to end one. The PCE opposed the wave of strikes in Madrid in the summer of 1936. For Díaz, see J. Estruch, *Historia del PCE 1920–1939*, volume 1 (Barcelona, 1978) p. 93. For the speech in its entirety, J. Díaz, *Tres Años de Lucha*, volume 1 (Barcelona, 1978) p. 241. For Thorez, F. Claudin, *The Communist Movement* (Harmondsworth, 1975) pp. 202–3.
27. *Guerra y Revolución en España 1936–1939*, volume 1 (Moscow, 1967) pp. 257–8.
28. Vidarte, *Todos Fuimos Culpables*, p. 477; Francisco Largo Caballero, *Notas Históricas de la Guerra en España 1917–1940*, volume 1, p. 257, Fundación Pablo Iglesias, Madrid; Américo Velez (pseud. José María Aguirre, politico-military secretary to Largo until May 1937) in *Informaciones*, 9 November 1977, Hemeroteca Nacional, Madrid. He states that Azaña's personal preference was for Prieto to form a government.
29. See above, note 11.
30. Bolloten, *The Spanish Revolution*, p. 121
31. For Azaña's reluctant acceptance, see his *Obras Completas*, volume III (Mexico, 1966–68) pp. 494–5, 501.
32. Prieto's speech, 'Intimidades confesadas en alta voz', *El Socialista* 1 February 1937.
33. L. Araquistain, *Claridad*, 10 April 1937.

34. See discussion of reports on the international situation presented by Jiménez de Asúa and Azorín at the PSOE National Committee meeting, 17–21 July 1937 in Valencia. Stenographic record (AH-24–2) pp. 44–5 in the PSOE's civil war archive, *Archivo Histórico de Moscú*, in the Fundación Pablo Iglesias, Madrid.
35. *El Socialista*, 11 September 1937. Throughout 1938 *El Socialista* editorials were increasingly vitriolic regarding the passivity of the two Socialist Internationals.
36. Amaro del Rosal, *Historia de la UGT*, volume 2, (Barcelona, 1977) pp. 550–1.
37. Gabriel Morón, *Política de Ayer y Política de Mañana* (Mexico, 1942) p. 243.
38. A. Vélez, *Informaciones*, 8 November 1977. For Araquistain's activities as republican ambassador in Paris, see Javier Tusell's introduction to *Luis Araquistain: Sobre la Guerra Civil y en la Emigración* (Madrid, 1983) pp. 24, 28–37.
39. Araquistain in a letter to Norman Thomas, Tusell, *Luis Araquistain*, pp. 51, 174.
40. *El Socialista*, editorial, 19 October 1937.
41. Bolloten, *The Spanish Revolution*, p. 187 and, for Largo's September cabinet, p. 122.
42. Ibid., pp. 185–90; for the November cabinet, ibid., pp. 189–90.
43. S. Juliá, *Orígenes del Frente Popular*, p. 161; G. Morón, *Política de Ayer*, pp. 71–3; Ramos Oliveira, *Historia de España*, volume 3, (Mexico, n.d.) p. 312.
44. M. Azaña, *Memorias Políticas y de Guerra* (Barcelona, 1978) p. 43; Vidarte, *Todos Fuimos Culpables*, p. 665.
45. For a reappraisal of the massive 'revolution versus war' debate and its implications, see R. Fraser, 'Reconsidering the Spanish Civil War', in *New Left Review*, no. 129, September–October 1981.
46. Largo Caballero to the Socialist Youth International, 8 May 1939, in *Exile Correspondence, Archivo Histórico de Moscú*. He defends the relations of the PSOE executive with the united youth organisation, the JSU, during the war, in that the latter's militants had acted as a brake on anarchist strength and had contributed to the consolidation of state power and to the building of a regular army.
47. Letter to Ben Tillett in Bolloten, *The Spanish Revolution*, p. 118; Reichmann interview in Vidarte, *Todos Fuimos Culpables*, p. 613.
48. Federico Urales' first letter is in *Adelante*, 12 January 1937; his second, plus Largo's reply, is in *El Socialista*, 12 February 1937.
49. Grandizo Munis, *Jalones de Derrota, Promesa de Victoria: Crítica y Teoría de la Revolución Española, 1930–1939* (repr. Madrid, 1977) pp. 358–9, 423.
50. Ibid., p. 414.
51. Morón, *Política de Ayer*, p. 71; UGT minutes, 15 September, 22 November, 17 December 1936.
52. Estruch, *Historia del PCE*, p. 106.
53. Morón, *Política de Ayer*, p. 79.
54. Prieto's speech at Egea de los Caballeros (Aragon) 19 May 1936, in Malefakis (ed.), *Discursos*, p. 282.

55. Bolloten, *The Spanish Revolution*, p. 341; Rodolfo Llopis in *Spartacus*, 1 October 1937.
56. Araquistain's own assessment of the May Days is in the note he published as ambassador in Paris, in *Correspondencia de Luis Araquistain*, Documentación Política, legajo 70/21, Archivo Histórico Nacional, Madrid; Bizcarrondo, *Araquistain y la Crisis Socialista* pp. 415–17.
57. Aldo Agosti, 'Alcance y límite de los Frentes Populares', in *Estudios de Historia Social*, no. 16–17, January – June 1981, p. 56; M. Bizcarrondo, *Araquistain y la Crisis Socialista*, p. 351.
58. Stalin's first letter is in *Guerra y Revolución en España*, volume 2, (Moscow, 1966) pp. 101–3, or Vidarte, *Todos Fuimos Culpables*, pp. 652–4. The second was delivered to Largo by hand by Marcelino Pascua, the Republic's ambassador in Moscow; see *El Socialista*, 12 February 1937, and Tusell, *Luis Araquistain*, p. 240.
59. J. Martínez Amutio, *Chantaje a un Pueblo* (Madrid, 1974) p. 215.
60. Vidarte, *Todos Fuimos Culpables*, pp. 668–9.
61. Ibid., p. 670.
62. Tuñón de Lara, *Historia de España*, volume IX (Barcelona, 1981) pp. 365–6; Ramón Lamoneda, 'Circular a los militantes del PSOE', August 1939, in *Posiciones Políticas* (Mexico, 1976) p. 227.
63. F. Jellinek, *La Guerra Civil en España* (Madrid, 1977) p. 465.
64. For an extremely brief but very positive reassessment of Negrín, see, S. Juliá, 'El Socialismo en busca de su historia', in *El País* (Libros) 5 December 1982; see also Vidarte, *Todos Fuimos Culpables*, p. 864; Jellinek, *La Guerra Civil*, p. 465.

7 Togliatti, Italian Communism and the Popular Front

Donald Sassoon

THE STRATEGY OF CLASS AGAINST CLASS

In July 1929 at the Tenth Plenum of the Executive Committee of the Communist International, Otto Kuusinen devoted his entire report to the so-called 'fascisation' of the socialist parties of the Second International. The final resolution indiscriminately identified as the main enemy 'capitalism, fascism, fascist social democracy including the MacDonald government which is a government of war and capitalist rationalization'.[1]

At this Plenum, which sanctioned Stalin's definitive victory within the Comintern, there was no real opposition or debate. The official target was social democracy, but there were also 'internal' targets: Bukharin and his friends in other parties. The obvious 'Bukharinite' in the Communist Party of Italy (PCI) was Angelo Tasca (pseudonyms: Serra and A. Rossi), one of the founders, with Antonio Gramsci, Palmiro Togliatti and Umberto Terracini, of the Ordine Nuovo group and of the PCI. Pressed by Togliatti (himself widely considered too close to Bukharin) Tasca later, on 30 August 1929, agreed that he had been 'at times mistaken' on Bukharin but insisted that the concept of the 'fascisation of social democracy' was 'substantially false'.[2]

Tasca's expulsion was inevitable. Kuusinen had threateningly told Togliatti to stop being 'tactful' with Tasca as he had been (mistakenly) with someone else, namely Trotsky.[3] Togliatti knew that after Stalin's victory nothing short of total acceptance of the new 'class against class' line would have satisfied the Soviet Communist Party. Consequently, at the Italian session of the Tenth Plenum he announced that he would drop the slogan of a constituent assembly and with it the entire strategy of intermediate phases between fascism and the proletarian dictatorship that he (and Gramsci) had devised: 'If the Comintern tells us that this is not right, we shall no longer pose these questions; we shall all think these things but we shall not speak of them; we shall only say that the anti-

131

fascist revolution and the proletarian revolution are one and the same thing'.[4]

That Togliatti would go on 'thinking these things' emerges clearly from the memoirs of Camilla Ravera, one of the leading members of the PCI. She recollects a meeting with Togliatti held shortly after the Tenth Plenum. Togliatti expressed the wish to leave politics: 'I am tired . . . I am not willing to say that our party's line has been wrong until now'.[5] Yet this was what was being asked not only by the Comintern but also by the younger generation of Italian communist leaders such as Luigi Longo.

Togliatti eventually decided to stay and, while upholding the new Comintern position, try to limit the damage it would do to the party. Togliatti remained cautious until he was sure that the Comintern had jettisoned the 'class against class' position in favour of the new Popular Front line.

Consequently, he broke with Bukharin, asserted there was no difference between social democracy and fascism, and condemned the slogan 'Towards a republican assembly', saying it should have been dropped sooner and more openly.[6]

By lining up with the Comintern and the young radicals within the party Togliatti cut himself off from the old Ordine Nuovo group, as Gramsci and Terracini, who were in jail, expressed their disagreement with the new line.[7]

Further expulsions followed that of Tasca's including that of Ignazio Silone. By then Togliatti had become an orthodox upholder of Comintern policy. At the Central Committee meeting of the PCI's youth federation in January 1930, he characterised the present situation thus:

(1) The capitalist crisis has reached the point at which the masses were bound to intervene openly and violently against the capitalist regime.
(2) The mass basis of fascism was about to disintegrate.
(3) Even though the crisis of fascism would generate anxieties within the bourgeoisie, the party should not assume that the bloc of landed interests and finance and industrial capital would break up or turn against fascism.[8]

'CLASS AGAINST CLASS' IN ITALY

As it turned out, Togliatti's predictions were quite wrong. However, because it was assumed that fascism was about to collapse, an entire levy of young and old militants – the best cadres of the party – were sent to Italy or 'activated' with the instruction to prepare for the imminent insurrection. At first this frenetic activism produced results: thousands of communist cadres coordinated the distribution of thousands of leaflets, newspapers and propaganda material, mainly in the north and in central Italy. The cost of all this, however, was enormous: the leading members of the newly reconstituted 'internal centre' of the party, including its head, Camilla Ravera, were arrested in July 1930, and hundreds of other arrests followed.[9] Nevertheless, the party was not destroyed but established itself as the leading anti-fascist force and supplanted the old Italian Socialist Party (PSI) in many regions, including traditional socialist strongholds such as the Emilia and Tuscany. The maximalist and reformist wings of the PSI joined forces in the so-called 'Anti-fascist Concentration' but, on the whole, the socialists were not very active in Italy and were mainly concerned with organising the emigrants. Within Italy, however, a new anti-fascist group had emerged: Giustizia e Libertà (GL). This was a radical organisation of intellectuals whose ideological ancestry could be traced back to Mazzini and the radical wing of the Risorgimento. GL was in favour of direct action including terrorism. In spite of these developments the official line of the PCI remained hostile to all other anti-fascist forces. At the Cologne Congress of the PCI in April 1931, the themes of the 'class against class' doctrine were forcefully reiterated, though it was apparent that there were fears that GL and its militant line might create some undesired competition.[10]

Togliatti took Giustizia e Libertà seriously enough to discuss it frequently. In September 1931 he wrote that many of GL's members were 'sincere anti-fascists' but most were 'ideologically confused and politically inexperienced'.[11] He saw GL as the most important attempt of the radical petty bourgeoisie to develop an independent line in order to take over the leadership of Italian anti-fascism.[12] Later that year Togliatti noted that socialists and GL were working together particularly within the Turin industrial working class. He warned the PCI to follow this activity with 'great care' in order to prevent its development 'which would be harmful to the mass movement'.[13] The party was then reminded that it was essential to win over, or at least influence, the GL rank-and-file.[14]

Thus the 'class against class' policy did not entirely prevent the development of contacts between communist activists and other anti-fascists. Gradually both GL and the PCI began to recognise the strength of their respective appeals and hence the contribution which each organisation could bring to the struggle against fascism. GL noted that the young were attracted to the PCI because of its organisation and its vision of radical social change, while the PCI recognised the strength of GL's slogan of 'justice and freedom'. In February 1932, Ruggero Grieco at a Central Committee meeting said: 'We would be very wrong if we believed that the masses do not care about the question of liberty . . . There is an economistic tendency within the party which has prevented us from linking the economic struggle with the struggle for freedom . . . The party must lead the struggle for freedom.'[15]

TOWARDS THE POPULAR FRONT

The attention given to the GL group, the renewed insistence that the 'class against class' strategy and the 'united front from below' line were not contradictory and the cautious espousal of general democratic slogans, all coexisted with the formal upholding of official Comintern policy. This began to change as the USSR sought to break its international isolation by signing non-aggression pacts with France and Poland in November 1932, and Italy in September 1933. However, it took Hitler's advent to power to modify not only the position of the Comintern but also that of the Socialist Second International (SI). In February 1933 the SI suggested an agreement on the struggle against fascism to the Comintern. Replying on 5 March 1933, the Comintern (pointedly noting the SI's new position) called on all 'communist parties to make a further attempt to establish a united fighting front with the social democratic working masses *through* the social democratic parties', (emphasis added).[16] It was the first time that, at least by implication, the Comintern had recognised the socialist parties as legitimate and representative working-class organisations.

The French communists (who, subsequently would be in the forefront of the development of the new Popular Front policy) approached the French socialists (the SFIO) on the following day, but to no avail. At that time the SI was in a 'centralist' phase and wanted negotiations between the two internationals and not between individual parties.[17] This was not acceptable to the Comintern and the negotiations between the PCF and the SFIO were temporarily abandoned.

The relations between the Italian communists and socialists reflected these developments closely. On 13 March Togliatti asked the PSI (but not GL) to form a united front but was rebuffed by the socialists who, like the French, followed the directives of the SI.[18] On the whole, however, the PCI remained faithful to the still-prevailing old line. This was due to the extreme weakness of the clandestine organisation of the party. The cadres it sent to Italy were regularly arrested. The PCI was frequently criticised by the Comintern for not being able to develop a strong anti-fascist movement in Italy. Its internal unity was precarious, as is usually the case with a party in difficulties. Togliatti was a very cautious man and knew that his party was not in a good position from which to wage a struggle for a change in policy.[19] Even as late as May 1934 the PCI continued to launch sectarian attacks against both the PSI and GL accusing their leaders of being 'pro-fascist'.[20] The PCI was thus not in the forefront of the battle for a change in the line of the Comintern. Yet, after the Nazi takeover, a change seemed increasingly inevitable. Dimitrov, the hero of the *Reichstag* fire trial, had arrived in Moscow in February 1934. He immediately pressed the case for a major change in the official line and was soon appointed to head work in the Comintern. This was a clear indication that Stalin supported the new strategy. For the PCI, however, the real turning-point was the pact of unity signed by the PCF and the SFIO on 27 July 1934. The climate of good-will which had arisen between French communists and socialists was particularly important to the PCI because it had influenced so many of its members who were immigrant workers in France. Togliatti himself was to recognise the importance of immigrant workers in his speech to the Comintern of 19 December 1933. In spite of all this, the road towards left unity in Italy was a slow one: it was not until July 1937, well after the Seventh Congress and three years after the PCF–SFIO pact, that the PCI and the PSI signed a pact of cooperation. It was to last until the late fifties.

THE TURNING-POINT IN FRANCE AND TOGLIATTI

In determining the main causes of this change it is difficult to assess the relative importance of direct Comintern intervention, internal changes in France or shifts in Soviet foreign policy. Nothing definitive will be written about this as long as the archives of the Comintern remain closed. Nevertheless, from what we do know it seems evident that the traditional view which characterises the Comintern as nothing more than a vehicle of Soviet foreign policy is far too mechanistic. A Franco–Russian entente could have been established without a change in the Comintern line. So at least two conditions were necessary for the green light to be given to the French Communist Party: favourable signals from Moscow, and pressures emanating from within the

Comintern itself, particularly from Dimitri Manuilsky and Dimitrov who were in turn opposed by Bela Kun and Pyatnitsky.[21] Claudín rightly points out that, 'We have no sufficient information to determine exactly how and why the decision was taken in May 1934' to change the official line of the PCF.[22] This does not stop him, a dozen pages later, from asserting that 'the national sections of the Comintern were totally subordinated to the policy of the Soviet state'.[23] Be that as it may, there is little doubt that there must have been some discussions within the Comintern as to whether the line should change or not. On 28 May 1934, the Presidium of the Comintern met to decide the agenda for its Seventh Congress. Hardliners such as Pyatnitsky, Knorin and Bela Kun were excluded from the list of main speakers (although they intervened in the debate), while Dimitrov was asked to give the main report and Togliatti the report on the international situation. Manuilsky too was included among the main speakers.

There is, however, no evidence that Togliatti had been in the forefront of the change in line. He did not have Dimitrov's prestige and must have been reluctant to keep a high profile. We are not even sure what exactly had been his role in the development of the French Popular Front. In his autobiography Maurice Thorez wrote that he himself took the initiative to include the Radical Party in the alliance:

I received, transmitted by the leader of a fraternal party, advice to abandon the formula and the idea of a People's Front. I replied that in a few minutes' time I was going to board the train for Nantes, and that I would there deliver a speech calling on the radicals to join in forming a People's Front.[24]

The leader of the fraternal party was Togliatti acting in his official Comintern capacity. Thorez, understandably desirous of stressing his political autonomy, does not mention what happened after the meeting. For this we have to turn to another source, the memoirs of Giulio Cerreti, an Italian communist who, having emigrated to France, had become a close aide of Thorez's and a member of the Central Committee of the French Communist Party. Cerreti confirms Thorez's account but adds that later that night Togliatti came to see him (Cerreti), told him he admired Thorez's political courage and urged him to go back to the French leader to tell him not to give up.[25] Togliatti was not uncritical of the PCF. He felt, for example, that the French were giving undue emphasis to negotiations at the top to the detriment of work among the masses.[26]

Though not an initiator of the Popular Front policy, Togliatti, once the new line had been accepted and he had ascertained that it had a good chance of success, attempted to develop it into an overall strategy for the transition to socialism. Unlike most of the other communist leaders he even tried to advance some mild and cautious criticisms of the previous policy lines of 'class against class' and 'united front from below': 'in the past . . . we have made concessions to sectarian tendencies, we have not fought them as it would have been necessary'.[27]

These self-critical remarks were never taken up by others nor did Togliatti develop them in a systematic way. The new Popular Front strategy was adopted without ever examining seriously the previous 'class against class' line. Togliatti was well aware that it would have been pointless to fight an internal battle he was bound to lose. He preferred instead to concentrate on three aspects of the new policy:

(1) The international dimension of the new popular front strategy.
(2) The 'mass' characteristic of popular frontism to ensure that it would not become a mere agreement between the leaderships of political parties.
(3) The application of such a policy to countries which had already been taken over by fascism. Here his attention was obviously focused on Italy.

These three aspects are discussed in turn.

THE INTERNATIONAL DIMENSION

This is the aspect of Togliatti's work in which, for understandable reasons, he departed least from the Soviet line. He was concerned that the new Popular Front policy should not be exclusively concerned with the national dimension but should be closely connected to the vicissitudes of international politics. The new policy was not aimed exclusively at blocking the advance of fascism in countries, such as France and Spain, which had maintained a democratic system. Its main aim was to ensure the isolation of Nazi Germany. In establishing these parameters Togliatti was acting as an authentic representative of international communism and of Stalin's Comintern. It is true that the Popular Front strategy was intended to give more autonomy to the national sections of the Third International but the principal guidelines had been set by developments in Soviet foreign policy. Nevertheless, the Popular Front was a genuine international strategy established by an international organisation for an international movement.

Togliatti would never overlook the foreign policy context of a national strategy and this principle was to guide him in the years to come when he would face the task of leading the largest communist party in the Western sphere of influence. The Popular Front policy was predicated upon the identification of a principal enemy against which it was necessary to coalesce all possible forces. For Togliatti, this was valid nationally and internationally and at the international level the main enemy was Nazi Germany. In a letter sent to the leadership of the PCI in April 1935, Togliatti criticised Thorez who had objected to the increase in French military expenditure: 'Maurice's speech must be criticised. It is a variation on the theme "the principal enemy is in our country". Today in the present situation it would be better to say that the principal enemy is German fascism poised against the USSR.'[28]

The doctrine of the 'principal enemy' in the field of international relations required an analysis which would systematically differentiate between the various imperialist countries. Togliatti's report to the Seventh Congress of the Third International highlighted the aggressive nature of German (and Japanese) imperialism, was critical of the role of Britain (accused of trying to entice Germany into attacking the USSR), and mild on the French bourgeoisie because 'it is intelligent enough to understand that national socialism [is a threat to] French national security'.[29] Togliatti concluded that Germany and Japan, encouraged by Britain, sought to create a coalition aimed at waging war against the USSR. This policy, however, would lead to a deterioration of the international situation and to a further differentiation between imperialist countries orientated towards the status quo and peace (led by France) and the bellicose ones such as Germany. Hence:

> war can erupt at any moment in this or that area and any war can become a world war. But the contradictions within the imperialist camp can develop in such a way . . . as to become obstacles to the creation of a coalition of countries seeking a war with the USSR.[30]

This analysis determined the main coordinates of Soviet foreign policy; but, added Togliatti, it must also determine the policies of the communist parties in the capitalist countries.[31] Thus there could be no contradiction between the national and the international application of the doctrine of the 'principal enemy'. To stop the war which was being prepared was the task of all members of the Comintern. In so doing they would be defending the USSR because:

> there is no doubt that the next war, even if it should begin as a war between two great imperialist powers or as a war by an imperialist

country against a small nation will inevitably become a war against the Soviet Union. Every year, every month gained will be for us too a guarantee that the Soviet Union will be stronger in fighting back against imperialism. Thus our policy of peace is directly linked to the policy of peace of the USSR.[32]

That the USSR and the international communist movement shared a main enemy (Nazi Germany) was particularly evident in the way Togliatti and the Comintern tackled the Ethiopian issue. Whenever 'the main enemy' was mentioned, it was always either Germany on its own or with Japan, but never with Italy. The invasion of Abyssinia was described by Togliatti in relatively dispassionate terms. He was particularly attentive to the international repercussions of the event and never indicated what sort of international action should be taken. In fact the Ethiopian question, which was the most important international issue of the day, did not figure very prominently at the Seventh Congress. There was no intervention specifically dealing with it and even Togliatti did not spend more than a couple of pages on Abyssinia. He did not discuss the attitude to be taken with respect to the League of Nations and the issue of sanctions against Italy, even though the Socialist International had already taken a stand in favour of sanctions on 31 July.[33]

What this demonstrates is that for Togliatti and the Comintern (it would be erroneous to suppose that Togliatti's report reflected only his own ideas) it was not inevitable that Italian and German fascism would end up by joining forces. Consequently it was necessary to avoid any action which might precipitate an Italo–German rapprochement. This was, of course, one of the main preoccupations not only of Soviet but also of French foreign policy. That, originally, had not been the position of the French and Italian Communist Parties. For both of them the Italian invasion of Ethiopia was the signal of the formation of a new fascist 'Holy Alliance'.[34]

In intervening as he had done at the Seventh Congress Togliatti may have been indicating to his comrades in the PCI that the situation determined by the invasion of Ethiopia was so complex and unstable that it was premature to take a definitive position. The strategy of the Popular Front did, of course, require the application of the 'doctrine of the principal enemy' to the wider international context but whether this 'principal enemy' had to be defined 'ideologically' – that is, fascism versus socialism and liberal democracy – or 'geopolitically' – that is, Nazi Germany versus the rest (including fascist Italy) – could not yet be resolved. It is this ambiguity which would permit the USSR to keep its options open and, eventually, with the Soviet–German pact, opt for temporary geopolitical security rather than for a clear-cut anti-fascist stand.

THE MASS DIMENSION: TOGLIATTI AND SPAIN

The mass dimension of the Popular Front had to be connected to and to some extent derived from the mass nature of fascism. We have already mentioned Togliatti's criticisms of the French Communist Party's tendency to reduce the new line to a question of an agreement at the top between the parties of the Left. In this section we examine in greater detail Togliatti's contribution to the analysis of fascism and how this links up with his view of the Popular Front and, in particular, with his considerations on the nature of the Spanish revolution.

In 1935 Togliatti gave a series of lectures on fascism at the party school in Moscow. He had already characterised the fascist party as a 'special type of party'.[35] This party does not work exclusively through the use of terror. It is not simply (as the Comintern definition implied) a terroristic dictatorship. Fascism has been able to create forms of organisation within the masses and to obtain some form of popular support: 'In the relation between the fascist dictatorship and the masses the important and characteristic aspect is the combination of violent methods and of terror with more or less compulsory forms of organisation of the masses created by the fascists themselves.'[36] In Togliatti's view the mass politics of fascism was a product of the crisis of 1929. Until then the primary task of fascism had been the destruction of the organisations of the masses. After 1929 this was no longer sufficient. The dangers of a mass movement against fascism were greater in a period of economic crisis.[37] Togliatti, in his lectures, analysed the various forms of fascist organisation and, in all cases, urged the Italian communists to participate in them and particularly in fascist trade unions:

> The fascist unions must not be regarded as a bloc without conflicts, without contradictions. The fascist unions represent a terrain on which we can see continual struggles unfold, on which we can see a constant modification of the class relations and of the forms of organisation.[38]

And later he added:

In exploiting the legal possibilities inside fascist unions, we must always remember how this organisation represents a body of class relations; and how it has been conceived in different ways by fascism in the various periods of fascism's development, and even in the same period, depending on the different situations which fascism has had to handle in various places.[39]

The kind of political work Togliatti envisaged was clearly distant from the 'class against class' strategy which emphasised the urgency of the crisis and the need for rapid mobilisation. In his writings of this period Togliatti was formulating a long haul strategy which depended on the patient construction of political relations throughout existing society, even a society organised by fascism. The principle of the 'long march through the institutions' was valid even when these institutions were fascist. This perspective is very close to the strategic thinking Antonio Gramsci was developing from the depths of his prison cell when, reflecting on the revolutionary process in the West, he put forward the theory of the 'war of position'. In an article Togliatti wrote in 1934 he explained that the reason why the PCI had not been able to stop fascism and was not properly equipped to fight it, was that the prevailing view in the party had been, and still was, that the struggle against fascism could only be a 'frontal attack'.

Nothing could be more mistaken. It is precisely because the fascist regime has a mass base and attempts to control the masses by regimenting them in organisations that the struggle against fascism, to be successful, must take into account the level at which the masses find themselves as well as the forms of organisation created by fascism. This requires not only dedication and heroism, but also flexibility, freedom of manoeuvre and the ability to modify rapidly one's form of organisation and work. These are all qualities we do not yet have.[40]

The long haul strategy, which Togliatti derived from the Popular Front line, implied a change in the assumption that the only progressive regime which could follow fascism was the dictatorship of the proletariat. The idea of intermediate phases, which Togliatti had been forced to drop at the Tenth Plenum of the Comintern, could once again be put forward. The main text in which this was done was 'Sulle particolarità della rivoluzione spagnola'. This was published on 24 October 1936 in Italian (in the *Grido del Popolo*), in French in *Correspondance Internationale* and in English in *Inprecorr*. Later that year it came out in pamphlet form in German and again in French.

Togliatti himself felt that this essay gave 'a theoretical basis to our position'.[41]

The bulk of Togliatti's essay was devoted to stressing all the peculiarities of what he called 'the Spanish revolution', that is the process which had begun with the victory of the Popular Front government and the consequent civil war. The international situation in which the war was being fought, the existence of internal 'national questions', the possibility offered by the war of eliminating the roots of Spanish fascism – all contributed to giving the Spanish revolution specific 'popular', 'national' and 'anti-fascist' features. Because of this 'it would not be correct to say that the Spanish revolution is identical to the Russian revolutions of 1905 or 1917. It has its own special and original features.'[42]

Togliatti went on to declare, 'It is not possible to explain the nature of the Spanish Popular Front by defining it simply as the democratic dictatorship of workers and peasants.'[43] Here he was implicitly taking issue with Dimitrov who, at the Seventh Congress of the Comintern, had stated that in those countries where fascism was not yet in power a Popular Front government 'may become the government of the democratic dictatorship of the working class and the peasantry'.[44] Togliatti's overall argument also developed in a way which implicitly contradicted Dimitrov's position on the question of the democratic stage between fascism and the dictatorship of the proletariat. In his report Dimitrov (quoting Lenin) had lashed out against the so-called 'right opportunists' who were trying:

> to establish a special 'democratic intermediate stage' between the dictatorship of the proletariat, for the purpose of instilling into the workers the illusion of a peaceful passage from one dictatorship to the other . . . Lenin spoke of the form of transition and approach to the *proletarian revolution*', that is, to the overthrow of the bourgeois dictatorship, and *not* some transitional form *between* the bourgeois and the proletarian dictatorships.[45]

For Dimitrov not only was there no transitional form of state but the united front government was seen very much as an instrument, as if it were only a temporary expedient designed to gain time to prepare for the real revolution. This is apparent when he said that the united front government could not bring 'final salvation' and 'remove the danger of fascist counter-revolution. Consequently it is necessary to *prepare for the socialist revolution!* Soviet power and *only* Soviet power can bring salvation!'[46]

In his own essay on Spain, Togliatti did not challenge Dimitrov directly. In the best Comintern style he quoted him as well as Lenin and Stalin (unusual for Togliatti who was not a quotation-monger) and then went on to state that the Spanish Popular Front was creating a 'new type of democratic republic' which was very unlike a bourgeois democratic republic, and that this republic, should it win the war, would have destroyed the material basis of fascism (something Dimitrov believed only Soviet power could achieve).[47]

Togliatti was able to examine more closely the evolution of the Spanish situation when, in July 1937, he went to Madrid as one of the main Comintern advisers to the Spanish Communist Party (PCE). He remained in Spain for twenty months, until the very end of the civil war. Certain documents from this period have recently emerged from the Comintern archives. They consist of five confidential letters sent to Dimitrov and Manuilsky at the Comintern in Moscow between the end of August 1937 and April 1938, a letter sent to the politburo of the PCE dated 12 March 1939; an appeal written for publication in the final days of the Spanish Republic; and a lengthy final report (sixty printed pages) written in Moscow after his return.

These documents show Togliatti in a frank, critical and less inhibited mood and somewhat modify the traditional image of Togliatti as one of the Comintern's leading hatchet men.[48]

Togliatti was very critical of the inability of the parties of the Popular Front to develop deeper links with the masses. On 30 August 1937 he wrote to Moscow: 'One has the impression that the government does not exist . . .'[49] and that '. . . it has no policy for the mobilisation of the masses in order to resolve political and economic problems . . .'[50] He complained of the lack of democracy in republican Spain:

> . . . as for the present organisation of political life in Spain in general: what is immediately evident is the absence of democratic institutions enabling the broad masses to participate in the political life of the country . . . In Spain now parliament represents no one . . . Local councils – the *ayuntamientos* – and the provincial councils are appointed from above . . . In the trade unions there is very little democracy . . . The political life of the country is outside of the control of the masses.[51]

He criticised the Spanish Communist Party particularly for its inability to forge links with rank-and-file anarchists or with their trade union (the CNT):

The party has not learned . . . to develop a Popular Front policy . . . it assumes that it is inevitable that all the other parties will eventually become anti-communist . . . The confusion has reached such a level that some comrades have even said that the principal task is 'the destruction of all capitalist elements'.[52]

He was scathing of the internal workings of the PCE, complaining that the leaders 'spend all day long talking to each other and to people who work in ministries or in the army', but they had no definite plan. 'Decisions are taken but no one checks whether they have been implemented.'[53] Togliatti then accused the Spanish communists of being sectarian with the anarchists, of not knowing the CNT, its leaders, or its internal problems. He wrote: 'I have not yet found a comrade able to tell me the names of the members of the CNT Executive Committee . . . there has been very little cooperation with the anarchists.'[54] He added that the PCE should 'try harder to work with the anarchists, to get closer to them', and suggested that CNT representatives should be included in the government[55] and, in November 1937, that there should be a pact between the PCE and the CNT.[56] Togliatti was also scathing about the way the Spanish communists worked in the trade unions. On 15 September 1937 he wrote to Dimitrov and Manuilsky and told them that the PCE did not understand what a mass line entailed. Its work in the unions was:

> not going well at all . . . What the comrades are interested in is the factional struggle within the unions . . . in this struggle they tend to care more for agreements at the top rather than the mobilisation of the masses for the protection of their own interests . . . There is very little work with the rank and file.[57]

Togliatti reserved his most outspoken contempt for some of the other Comintern advisers. He clearly objected to their excessive interference in the internal life of the PCE. Shortly after his arrival he wrote, on 30 August 1937, that 'the responsibility for the poor work the party is doing rests at least in part with our advisers. It is necessary to convince L. [Louis, i.e. Vittorio Codovila] to change his methods radically . . . L. must stop being the one in whose absence no one dares to take any decisions'.[58] He renewed his criticisms in his next report (15 September):

> it is necessary to change radically the way in which our 'advisers' work. There are comrades here (Uribe, Dolores, Hernández, Giorla) who can run the party and run it well . . . Your 'advisers' must stop

thinking that they are the party bosses and that the Spanish comrades are worth nothing.[59]

Togliatti had become increasingly displeased with Codovila: 'Louis's *presence here harms the party* . . . My opinion is that we have made a very serious mistake to put the PCE under the tutelage of L.'[60] Obviously the hated Louis had some powerful friends in Moscow because in his report of 25 November 1937 Togliatti was clearly exasperated: '*Louis*: I am not happy with his presence here. I do not know whether you tried to make him understand his mistakes. In any case he has not understood them . . . His presence here *makes my work more difficult*.'[61]

Excessive control on the part of the Comintern, however, did not figure among the causes of the republican defeat listed by Togliatti in his long Moscow report of 21 May 1939. Nevertheless he renewed many of the criticisms made in the course of his stay. In particular he stated that 'throughout the war there has never been a real democratic regime'.[62] As for the PCE, it had never been able to establish proper links with the anarchist-influenced Barcelona proletariat, nor the socialist rank-and-file in Madrid. It had failed to organise the masses outside the parties, to develop the trade unions, to educate their own cadres, or to develop a self-critical outlook: 'In the party there was always more pride than critical spirit'.[63]

The principal causes of the defeat were not traced by Togliatti to the strategy itself but to the fact that the internal and external alliance system it presupposed never materialised. Internationally, French and British non-intervention policies objectively favoured the joint intervention of Germany and Italy; internally there was never sufficient unity within the Popular Front itself – the working class was deeply divided (socialists, communists and anarchists), there was no democracy, no proper political work in areas under Francoist occupation and no adequate struggle against traitors in the republican areas.[64]

On the whole, the most important experiment of Popular Front in a country where an authoritarian or fascist regime had not already been established had failed miserably. It is necessary to look at developments in Italy after the Seventh Congress in order to examine the application of the Popular Front strategy in a fascist country.

THE POPULAR FRONT AND ITALIAN FASCISM

For the Italian communists the Popular Front could not be reduced to an alliance between the anti-fascist parties. It was always clear that, by itself, this alliance could not bring about the defeat of fascism. Of the three leading anti-fascist parties (the PCI, the PSI and GL), the PCI had the best organisation but, until the war, it was never in a position to endanger in the slightest degree the stability of fascism. GL had the best contacts with the intellectuals but their practical activity could never be more than the occasional distribution of illegal material and an act of sabotage from time to time. As for the PSI it hardly mattered.

By 1935, Togliatti, though no longer directly in charge of the PCI, was still regarded as the real leader. While Togliatti was in Moscow as a member of the Secretariat of the Comintern and head of its 'Latin' section, Ruggero Grieco was in charge of the Politburo of the PCI.

The operative principles the party had to follow had been enunciated by Togliatti himself in August 1935: 'In countries where there is a fascist dictatorship or a large fascist movement we must involve the broad masses of "fascist" workers in the struggle and organise them. For as long as we are not able to do so, the chances for the united front will not be good.'[65] Togliatti assumed that the first weakening in the fascist regime would not be the result of the actions of the anti-fascist movement but would come from within the 'fascist masses'.[66] It followed that the primary task of the PCI was to facilitate the development of an internal opposition to fascism:

> The problem can be put like this. There is an (openly) anti-fascist opposition, mainly made up by the remnants of the old anti-fascist parties and active abroad. But a new opposition, which we shall call 'fascist', is developing within the country. This could rapidly become an important force. Between these two oppositions there are no links. . . . We must create them. Hence the old anti-fascist parties must change their positions. If we speak to (real) fascists who are discontented or indignant and want something new and we talk to them about . . . Matteotti, they would beat us up. Could they be approached differently, not by rejecting them but by seeking a way in which they could join up with us? . . . It is the task of our party to find this way. Only our party . . . can succeed in the task of achieving *the unity of all the oppositions to fascism. This is now for us the problem of the popular front.*[67]

Thus the Popular Front in Italy meant the development of new forms of cooperation not only with the anti-fascist parties (as was the case, for example, in France), but also with 'fascist' dissidents. Togliatti suggested that the slogan of the Constituent Assembly should be dropped and that propaganda should be more anti-capitalist than anti-fascist.[68] He warned against a mechanical application of the line of the Seventh Congress[69] and continued to insist that all efforts should be made to win over the masses influenced by fascism.[70]

The party's external centre, situated in Paris, followed these directives but, as we shall see, with excessive zeal. In the summer of 1936 it produced an appeal called 'For the Salvation of Italy, for the Reconciliation of the Italian People'. Known as 'the appeal to the brothers in blackshirts' it was signed by virtually all party leaders including Togliatti. It read, in part: 'Fascist worker! To you we offer our hand because with you we want to build an Italy of peace and labour; we offer our hand because, like you, we are sons of the people, we are your brothers, we have the same interests and enemies.'[71]

The appeal was extended to Catholics and socialists, contained no reference to Mussolini, did not attack fascism but singled out as the main enemy, listing them by name, the twenty or so richest and most powerful Italian families. It was in fact an attempt to use the propaganda of the French Communist Party, including the themes of 'reconciliation' and the 'two hundred families' who allegedly ran the country. Togliatti had not written the appeal but there is no evidence that he objected to the inclusion of his name. Some members of the Politburo of the PCI attempted to go even further than the appeal. Mario Montagnana suggested: 'We must have the courage to say that we do not aim to destroy fascism: we cannot do it now. The 1919 fascist programme which we should adopt presupposes the existence of fascism not its end.'[72] Grieco and others did not agree with this position and said it was 'opportunistic', but eventually a compromise was reached in September 1936 with a resolution which met Montagnana's position more than half-way. However, this understandably provoked the dismay of both the PSI and GL who reminded the Italian communists of the 'ideological, political and social gap which separates us from fascism'.[73]

Togliatti, who had approved the general principles of the resolution of September 1936, tried to rectify the situation by insisting that the struggle for democracy had to remain the primary objective and that 'reconciliation' had to be with the Italian people and not with fascism.[74] Only in February 1937 would Togliatti take a clear stand against the Montagnana position: the PCI had to involve the masses influenced by fascism in the struggle, but the aim was still the destruction of the fascist regime.[75]

The truth of the matter, however, was that this development, though it made the PCI more flexible politically and thus equipped it for the resistance of 1943–45, could not have an immediate impact. The PCI did not possess the resources, the personnel or the apparatus with which to carry out any major activities against fascism in this period. In April 1938, from Moscow, Manuilsky accused the PCI of being infiltrated at all levels and mistaken in its approach to the Popular Front policy. The Comintern decided to dissolve the PCI's Central Committee and to create a new smaller one (only eight members). Grieco was ousted and Giuseppe Berti, who had been the most outspoken of all the PCI leaders in his criticism of the PCI position, was put in charge of the party's organisation.[76]

Moscow's criticisms did not subside. At the Eighteenth Congress of the Soviet Communist Party on 17 March 1939 Manuilsky, though he praised the German Communist Party, launched into a bitter attack on the PCI for its inability to develop any kind of mass struggle against fascism. By then Soviet policy was moving rapidly towards the non-aggression pact with Germany. By itself this would not modify sensibly the line of the PCI (as it would that of the PCF): the main enemy remained Italian fascism.

It was only after the disintegration of Mussolini's regime itself in 1943 that the PCI would be able to form a broad Popular Front and lead the Italian resistance. Then and only then, with the return of Togliatti from exile in 1944, would the most fruitful lessons of the Seventh Congress be applied. The experience Togliatti and the Italian communists had gained in the difficult inter-war years would lead them to develop a new line of advance towards socialism which would go beyond the Seventh Congress. This became an original 'Italian road to socialism' which would eventually enable the PCI to become the largest communist party in the capitalist world.

Notes

1. J. Degras (ed.), *The Communist International 1919–1943: Volume 3, 1929–1943* (London, 1971) p. 66.
2. Giuseppe Berti, *I Primi Dieci Anni di Vita del PCI. Documenti Inediti dell'Archivio Angelo Tasca* (Milan, 1967) pp. 510–12.
3. P. Spriano, *Storia del Partito Comunista Italiano. Volume II, Gli Anni della Clandestinità* (Turin, 1969) p. 215.
4. P. Togliatti, E. Ragionieri (ed.), *Opere*, Volume II (Rome, 1972) p. 794.
5. C. Ravera, *Diario di Trent'Anni 1913–1943* (Rome, 1973) p. 449.
6. P. Togliatti, E. Ragionieri (ed.), *Opere*, Volume III, Tome i (Rome, 1973) p. 103. See also Ragionieri's introduction, p. xlviii.

7. See Athos Lisa, 'Discussione politica con Gramsci in carcere', *Rinascita*, 12 December 1964; U. Terracini, *Sulla Svolta. Carteggio Clandestino dal Carcere 1930–31–32* (Milan, 1975) pp. 9–10; and A. Davidson, *The Theory and Practice of Italian Communism* (London, 1982) p. 198.

8. Togliatti, *Opere*, III, i, p. 134.

9. Spriano, *Storia, II*, p. 291.

10. Ibid., p. 319.

11. P. Togliatti, 'Sul movimento di Giustizia e Libertà', in *Lo Stato Operaio*, September 1931, in *Opere*, III, i, p. 411.

12. Ibid., p. 413.

13. Ibid., p. 427.

14. Ibid., p. 434.

15. Spriano, *Storia, II*, p. 350.

16. Degras, *The Communist International*, p. 253.

17. E. H. Carr, *The Twilight of the Comintern 1930–1935* (London, 1982) pp. 85–6.

18. Spriano, *Storia, II*, pp. 377–8.

19. How distrusted the PCI was in Moscow emerges clearly from E. H. Carr, *The Twilight of the Comintern*, pp. 239–55.

20. G. Amendola, *Storia del Partito Comunista Italiano 1921–1943* (Rome, 1978) p. 231.

21. B. Leibzon and K. Shirinya, *Povorot v Politike Kominterna* (Moscow, 1975). The Italian translation used here is V. M. Lejbzon and K. K. Sirinja, *Il VII Congresso dell'Internazionale Comunista* (Rome, 1975). These authors give the PCF the main credit for the turning-point in France.

22. F. Claudín, *The Communist Movement. From Comintern to Cominform* (Harmondsworth, 1975) p. 175.

23. Ibid., p. 187.

24. Quoted in Claudín, *The Communist Movement* p. 688. The passage can be found in Maurice Thorez, *Fils du Peuple* (Paris, 1960) p. 102.

25. Giulio Cerreti, *Con Togliatti e Thorez* (Milan, 1973) pp. 168–72.

26. See the letter he sent from Paris to Manuilsky on 19 November 1934, lengthy extracts from which are quoted in Ernesto Ragionieri's introduction to Togliatti, *Opere*, III, i, p. cxci.

27. 'Problemi del fronte unico' in *Lo Stato Operaio*, 8 August 1935, now in Togliatti, *Opere*, III, ii, p. 717.

28. Quoted in Paolo Spriano, *Il Compagno Ercoli* (Rome, 1980) p. 26.

29. Togliatti, *Opere*, III, ii, pp. 754–5.

30. Ibid., p. 756.

31. Ibid., p. 757.

32. Ibid., pp. 765–6.

33. See the detailed discussion in G. Procacci, *Il Socialismo Internazionale e la Guerra d'Etiopia* (Rome, 1978) pp. 104*ff*.

34. Ibid., pp. 86–90.

35. P. Togliatti, 'Dov'è la forza del fascismo italiano', *L'Internationale Communiste*, no. 19, 5 October 1934, now in Togliatti, *Opere*, III, ii, pp. 470–1. See also P. Togliatti, *Lectures on Fascism* (London, 1976) pp. 13–27 in which this concept is further discussed.

36. Togliatti, *Opere*, III, ii, p. 476. See also p. 478 showing his list of the

following fascist organisations: the Fascist Party, fascist youth, the Balilla, university students, teachers, civil servants, workers in the public sector, the railwaymen, the post office workers, the trade unions, the *dopolavoro* and the mutual aid societies.

37. Togliatti, *Lectures on Fascism*, p. 26.
38. Ibid., p. 64.
39. Ibid., p. 71.
40. P. Togliatti, 'Considerazioni sul 30 giugno', *Lo Stato Operaio*, July 1934, now in Togliatti, *Opere*, III, ii, p. 410.
41. Spriano, *Il Compagno Ercoli*, p. 79.
42. P. Togliatti, Franco Andreucci and Paolo Spriano (eds), *Opere 1935–1944*, volume IV, tome i (Rome, 1979) p. 140.
43. Ibid., p. 151.
44. Georgi Dimitrov, *Report to the 7th Congress Communist International 1935. For the Unity of the Working Class Against Fascism* (London, 1973) p. 128.
45. Ibid., pp. 97–9.
46. Ibid., pp. 98–9.
47. Togliatti, *Opere*, IV, i, p. 152. For a different, and in this author's view mistaken, reading of this text see Claudín, *The Communist Movement*, p. 214.
48. This negative view is largely based on Jesús Hernández, *Yo Fue un Ministro de Stalin en España* (1953), a notoriously unreliable book described as an 'unpleasant work' in Hugh Thomas, *The Spanish Civil War* (London, 1961) p. 217. This does not deter Thomas from relying heavily on Hernández.
49. Togliatti, *Opere*, IV, i, p. 260.
50. Ibid., pp. 263–4.
51. Ibid., pp. 264–5.
52. Ibid., p. 267.
53. Ibid., pp. 270–1.
54. Ibid., pp. 268–9.
55. Ibid., p. 270.
56. Ibid., p. 289.
57. Ibid., pp. 276–7.
58. Ibid., pp. 271–2. Codovila was an Argentine communist of Italian origin, and Comintern adviser in Spain since 1933. He was also known as 'Comrade Medina'. After the Second World War he became the leader of the Argentinian Communist Party.
59. Ibid., p. 274.
60. Ibid., pp. 278–9.
61. Ibid., p. 291.
62. Ibid., p. 405.
63. Ibid., pp. 408–9.
64. Ibid., pp. 404–6.
65. Togliatti, *Opere*, III, ii, p. 722.
66. 'Letter to the Secretariat of the PCI', October 1935, now in Togliatti, *Opere*, IV, i, p. 25.
67. Ibid., p. 26.
68. Ibid., p. 28.
69. Letter to Ruggero Grieco, 26 October 1935, in Togliatti, *Opere*, IV, i, p. 31.

70. See, among others, his article of 15 November 1935, in Togliatti, *Opere*, IV, i, pp. 55–6; and his intervention to the Presidium of the Executive Committee of the Comintern, 5 February 1936, in ibid., p. 93.
71. Spriano, *Il Compagno Ercoli*, p. 62.
72. Cited in ibid., p. 65.
73. Ibid., p. 66.
74. Ibid., p. 67 and P. Spriano, *Storia del Partito Comunista Italiano. Volume III, I Fronti Popolari. Stalin, la Guerra* (Turin, 1970) p. 99.
75. Spriano, *Il Compagno Ercoli*, p. 70.
76. Spriano, *Storia del Partito Communista Haliana*, p. 249.

8 The Soviet Union, the Comintern and the Demise of the Popular Front 1936–39

Jonathan Haslam

This chapter is an interpretative presentation which is not intended as a comprehensive account of the events under discussion; that would require a volume of its own. Furthermore, many of the answers to our questions are still hidden from view. Although we now have a fairly accurate picture of Soviet diplomacy during these troubled years, thanks to the opening of Western foreign ministry archives and the publication of selections from the Soviet diplomatic correspondence (the *Dokumenty Vneshnei Politiki SSSR*), the domestic political history of the USSR from 1929 until Stalin's death in 1953 is still *terra incognita*; and if it is difficult (though not impossible) to separate out the history of Soviet diplomacy from the domestic politics of the USSR, it is all the more foolhardy to treat Comintern history apart from the Byzantine politics of the Stalin period, particularly during the years of the Terror from 1936 to 1939: the years under discussion here.

By 1936 the Comintern was set firmly on the path laid down at the Seventh Congress in August 1935: that of the Popular Front. The strategy of the Popular Front originated in the response of the French Communist Party (PCF) to the growing threat of fascism in the autumn of 1934 – an heretical improvisation adopted by Moscow only with deep reservations. Its adoption coincided with a period of increasing liberalisation in Soviet society which had only momentarily and partly been jeopardised by the mysterious (and still unexplained) assassination of the popular Leningrad Party Secretary, Sergei Kirov, in December 1934. After the traumatic upheaval of the enforced collectivisation of agriculture and the enormous sacrifices associated with the achievement of the first five-year plan of industrialisation (1929–32), the new breeze of liberalisation came as a welcome breath of fresh air. The shift in Comintern strategy also coincided with the growing cosmopolitanism of Soviet diplomacy. Under People's Commissar of Foreign Affairs,

Maxim Litvinov, Soviet diplomacy worked towards the collective containment of Nazi Germany. The policies of the Popular Front and of collective security were both similar responses to the same threat. By the end of August 1939, however, all three policies, domestic and foreign – Popular Front, collective security and domestic liberalisation – were dead; only the Popular Front had yet to be laid out for burial. Although each policy succumbed at different stages, it is not implausible to raise the issue as to whether the demise of all three was not in some sense interrelated, rooted in a common cause, a product of the same dynamic.

The inauguration of the Popular Front strategy in 1935 not only heralded an end to the tragic sectarianism of the preceding – so-called 'third' – period in Comintern policy, it also implied a greater degree of democracy within the international communist movement: a greater degree of autonomy for member communist parties. As part of the movement to unite the anti-fascist forces within their national boundaries, individual sections were encouraged to identify more closely with national institutions previously scheduled for future demolition; the leader of the PCF, Maurice Thorez, even extended a hand to the Catholic Church (*la main tendue*). In this sense the Popular Front strategy presaged the kind of autonomy sought by certain leading communist parties – and the Italian Communist Party (PCI) in particular – from 1944–47 and, again and more successfully, from 1956–57 and in the 1970s. But in the thirties this trend was more than counterbalanced by rival forces which had resulted from the threat of fascism as much as had the Popular Front strategy. In the face of an overwhelming need for unity against the fascist threat, the Comintern General Secretary, Georgii Dimitrov, and his like-minded comrades were even more concerned to ensure that all parties adopted and effectively implemented the chosen strategy – even Asian parties – than to shake off the old habits of directing tactics centrally from Moscow. When the issue arose in the form of choosing between the alternatives of either laissez-faire and possible breaches in the Popular Front, or outside interference and orthodoxy to the Popular Front line, Dimitrov and his followers necessarily elected for centralisation and uniformity. Furthermore, the Comintern was not only based in Moscow but also totally dependent upon the Soviet regime for its sustenance and continued existence. As far as Stalin was concerned, its member parties had failed in their initial task of relieving the isolation of the Soviet Union by launching successful revolutions in their own countries; their only value to him was as another arm of Soviet state interests abroad. The idea of a more liberal Comintern regime was thus never really practicable because, like it or not, Comintern activity was supposed to serve – however indirectly – the interests of the Soviet regime. These restrictions were apparent even before the wave of liberalisation came to an end in the Soviet Union (1935–36). During that period, provided it did not step on too many governmental toes in Moscow, the Comintern was free to plough its own furrow. But when liberalisation came to an abrupt and bloody end in the summer of 1936, the Comintern found itself defenceless against the police onslaught the following winter (1936–37).

The summer of 1936 was a period of crisis for both domestic and foreign policies in the Soviet Union. Firstly, the movement towards greater constitutionality in government, which had begun hesitantly with the re-introduction of 'socialist legality' in the countryside in 1933, had reached its peak by June 1936 with the discussion of a new constitution. The years of crisis (1929–32) over, criticism of Stalin as party leader had grown rather than diminished, and some even looked upon the coming constitution as the prelude to greater political democratisation. The old left opposition – its scattered remnants – had found common cause with the former right opposition (Bukharin as its figurehead) in criticising Stalin's personal abuse of power. Young Communists listened eagerly to the tales of Old Bolsheviks about 1917. They were restless at the evident bourgeoisification of Soviet society: concessions to the peasantry, piece-rate systems at work, the re-introduction of officers' ranks etc. They were also uneasy at and critical of alliances with capitalist states (France and Czechoslovakia in 1935) and the drift towards social reformism in the Comintern (the Popular Front). By the summer of 1936, discontent – scarcely insurrectionary and as yet merely talk – had evidently reached a level intolerable to Stalin, ever suspicious (and not unjustifiably so) that others wished to unseat him from power. Early in June 1936, foreign events intruded and further reinforced disquiet at the direction Soviet foreign policy (including Comintern policy) had taken.

After a successful election for the Popular Front in allied France, the workers of Paris occupied the factories in a manner reminiscent of the metallurgical workers in Turin in 1920. From his place of exile the exultant Leon Trotsky, hounded from the Soviet Union in 1929, heralded the coming of the French Revolution. This was arguably a disaster for the Soviet policy of collective security, founded as it was upon cooperation with existing governments rather than upon the forces of revolution. In Moscow the Commissariat of Foreign Affairs (*Narkomindel*) had been alarmed at the successes of the PCF in the elections which brought the Popular Front to power for fear it would alienate the Centre and scare the Right, thus ultimately jeopardising the future of the Franco–Soviet alliance. The occupation of the factories came as even worse news. Chaos in the capital of the only great power which had allied with the USSR (with grave misgivings and in spite of warnings from Britain) was hardly the best advertisement for prospective marriages of convenience with others. Furthermore, anything which re-awakened longstanding British suspicions of the Bolsheviks would only weaken the chances of drawing the British government into the encirclement of Nazi Germany. Indeed the '*évènements*' in France alerted bourgeois Europe to the fact that Bolshevism was alive and well, that private property was no more secure than it had been at the end of the First World War, and suggested to many that perhaps fascism was – for all its faults – the lesser menace. The outbreak of the Spanish Civil War in late July 1936, which resulted in a revolution from below on the part of workers and peasants, confirmed such fears. The fact that the Russians had nothing directly to do with either crisis mattered little. Stalin was in fact caught in an insoluble dilemma: the 'Left' in the USSR blamed him for doing nothing to aid the rising revolutions in the West; the conservative powers of Europe blamed the uprisings on Bolshevik machinations. Abroad Stalin was accused of being a revolutionary; at home he was accused of being a counter-revolutionary. With PCF leader Thorez counselling French workers on the importance of knowing how to end a strike, it certainly looked as though the Comintern was going the way of the pre-war Second International. Trotsky said as much, and his ideas acquired new resonance in Russia. The dilatory and initial half-hearted response to the Spanish Civil War, then the adoption by the Soviet government of French proposals for non-intervention in August, caused even the highly cynical Karl Radek to declare the need for Soviet intervention on the grounds not of Soviet state interests but of proletarian internationalism. To all intents and purposes Radek had long ago buried his principles when he betrayed the opposition at the end of the 1920s. The fact that even he now stood up in the name of revolutionary internationalism is some indication of the extent to which Stalin appeared to be losing his grip in Moscow.

The threat to Stalin's dictatorship was thus inextricably linked to Comintern issues as well as domestic political reform. Inevitably Stalin's counter-attack would also be directed against those who stood for revolutionary internationalism as against *raison d'état*. Against this background, the trial of former oppositionists, Zinoviev and Kamenev, in late August 1936, acquired significance as a clear warning to those who had come to believe that Soviet politics were open to public participation, or that pressure from below would change policies decided at the top, or that Leninist norms for party democracy were on the verge of reinstatement. The trial was the ominous prelude to the destruction of all existing and potential foci of opposition to Stalin's personal supremacy. After August 1936 nothing would ever be the same again, and this applied to the Comintern as much as, if not more than, to the rest of the Soviet state apparatus, the party and Soviet society, from which the Comintern was only formally and notionally divorced. Not only had the Comintern been associated with the demand for intervention in Spain, but from the very beginning the sources of opposition were crudely identified with the foreign menace and any campaign of xenophobia would inevitably prove crippling to the Comintern, which was staffed almost entirely by foreigners – that 'nest of spies', as the NKVD referred to it. People began to disappear from the Comintern apparatus at an alarming rate: *'takovo u nas nyet'* (there is no such person here) was the all too common response to those returning from abroad who phoned colleagues and friends in the organisation.

Spain was significant not only as a trigger in Stalin's decision to move decisively against dissentient opinion, but also as the most important test for the Popular Front strategy in Europe and as an example of how the terror unleashed within the USSR undermined Comintern strategy abroad. Spain revealed the two contradictory faces of Soviet power: its progressive role as a rallying point for democrats against fascism, but also its own grim visage as an arbitrary despotism. Having moved to liquidate former oppositionists, future oppositionists and imaginary oppositionists at home, Stalin compromised his government's official support for non-intervention in Spain by sanctioning the export of armaments to the Republic and by unleashing the Comintern to galvanise world support for aid to the republican cause. As ever, Stalin adopted the policy of his opponents (in this case Radek and others) as he moved to secure their liquidation. Along with the small army of 'advisers' sent to Spain went a number of men from the NKVD who arrived with an equation between 'Trotskyists' and fascists already firmly implanted in their minds. The civil war within the Spanish Civil War, between the communists and moderate socialists on the one hand and the non-communist revolutionaries (including the anarchists) on the other, only confirmed those conducting the terror in Russia in their belief that the enemy lay within.

To attribute to all this the collapse of the Spanish Republic is to overlook more obvious causes: in particular the massive scale of aid to

Franco and his forces from Italy and Germany; also the fact that in exporting this mode of terror to Spain, the Russians were still not responsible for creating the divisions on the Left. These divisions were already deep-seated. Moreover, Soviet aid made a tremendous contribution to the relief of Madrid in November–December 1936 and, with the arrival of the artful Togliatti in July 1937 to take control of Communist Party (PCE) operations, the Comintern made new and repeated efforts to heal the wound opened by the battles behind the lines in Barcelona early that year. Yet for all that, the Popular Front failed and in March 1939 the Republic fell to Franco. It was a cruel fact of life that since July 1936 the Right was far more unified than the Left; that the revolutionary upsurge had terrified the Right into unity while simultaneously failing to carry a revolution to fruition (a phenomenon not unfamiliar to the rest of Europe); that Popular Front policies (*la main tendue* etc.) tended to accentuate the splits in the Left rather than heal the divisions, by pointing up the differences between those who sought immediate revolution and those whose primary aim was the restoration of the status quo *ante bellum*; that apart from Russia no other great power would aid the Republic; that Soviet aid was ever insufficient, not least for lack of a powerful navy to protect it en route and because unrestricted passage through uncertain France was only intermittent at a time when German and Italian aid to the rebels was unstinting.

Spain proved a failure. France was little more successful. There the Popular Front ran aground on the contradictions inherent in French conditions. As the '*évènements*' of June 1936 had demonstrated, there was pressure for revolution from below. The PCF sought to contain those pressures while using them as leverage on the Popular Front government in order to obtain material concessions for the working class. However, the PCF was always awkwardly sandwiched between demands from below, voiced through the trade unions, and demands from above, voiced by its allies in the Socialist and Radical Parties. Refused permission to join the Popular Front government by Moscow, the PCF adopted a policy of conditional support for the regime which proved insufficiently helpful to the government in terms of easing its domestic and foreign policy dilemmas, yet at the same time was insufficiently radical to appease the revolutionary elements. What is so striking is that during this period, still very much under Moscow's tutelage and despite mass popular support within France, the PCF appears to have been strikingly ineffective as a force for change in French politics after 1936.

Why did the PCF prove so ineffective? Moscow's veto over communist participation in the French government certainly circumscribed the ability of the PCF to shift policy in its direction, although participation might merely have further circumscribed the PCF with greater responsibility and complicity without producing any greater impact on policy formation. As it was, PCF agitation on issues resolved unsatisfactorily by successive administrations – not least the failure to aid the Spanish Republic – highlighted the divisions on the Left; but it does not of itself explain those divisions which, as in Spain, originated long before the advent of fascism.

Across the board, association with Stalin's rule of terror made the position of all European communist parties that much more difficult; it weakened the case for the Popular Front, since it exacerbated suspicions on the left and in the centre that, should the communists attain power, a bloodbath might well engulf them. The terror gave those who opposed close association with the communists (as in the British Labour Party) on other grounds a plausible argument against those pressing for unity with Comintern sections. The terror scythed its way through the entire contingent of Polish communists in Moscow. This was the most extreme example of the extent of the repression in which even Togliatti's brother-in-law was tortured. The Poles were traditionally intimates with the Soviet Communist Party. Ironically they provided the early leaders of the Cheka and also the earliest victim within the leadership of the international movement – Sochacki, who was arrested and imprisoned for espionage in 1932 (he was later rehabilitated). The position of the Poles was undoubtedly worsened by the fact that the regime of Colonel Beck obstructed all Soviet efforts in Eastern Europe to contain the expansion of Nazi Germany and was therefore identified as an ally of the Germans. It was therefore a fairly simple matter for the NKVD to fabricate a web of conspiracy to justify the wholesale liquidation of the Polish Communist Party in emigration. The party was formally dissolved in 1938.

On the Soviet side, the failure of the Popular Front to accomplish much more than a temporary and very imperfect holding action against the spread of fascist/German influence across Europe was only too evident as the thirties drew to a close. By the autumn of 1938, the Russians were isolated in world diplomacy by a Britain bent on the appeasement of Nazi Germany. Along with the terror, a sense of disappointment and then bitterness had undercut the re-emergent internationalism of the Seventh Congress. By the time of the Munich settlement at the end of September 1938, the fate of both the collective security and Popular Front experiments had underlined the fact that, whether in the field of diplomacy or the field of Comintern activity, a multilateral solution to Soviet security simply did not exist. For lack of any feasible alternative – mere withdrawal into isolation would have proved fatal – these policies were continued into 1939 until their bankruptcy was made evident by the failure to secure an alliance on satisfactory terms from Britain and France and by the new shift in Germany policy towards a Russo–German condominium in Eastern Europe. The resultant pact with Germany achieved on the 23 August 1939 did not cause an immediate reversal of Comintern policy, but the reasons for this do not lie in some fictitious notion of Comintern autonomy. Not until Stalin was certain that Hitler would fulfil the conditions of the pact concerning the division of Poland would he neutralise the Popular Front as a tool of Soviet policy; and that was finally effected only with the signature of the Soviet–German friendship pact at the end of September 1939.

The Popular Front policy had been ushered into the Comintern as a result of pressure from the ranks. It was acceptable to Stalin because it complemented – or so it seemed – the diplomatic effort to contain Nazi Germany; though the friction between the two lines soon became apparent in France and elsewhere. It proved dangerous to Soviet policy when the Russians moved towards a condominium with Nazi Germany in 1939 and was therefore demolished at a stroke. It was revived in June 1941 when the condominium broke with the Nazi invasion of the USSR. Not much should be expected of a policy so self-evidently tailored to suit Soviet state interests. In order for communist parties to have pursued the Popular Front with any credibility they would have had to dissociate themselves from Soviet tutelage, and that was simply out of the question in the thirties.

Like it or not, the fate of the Popular Front was bound up with the direction of the Comintern. The Comintern's role as an arm of the Soviet regime meant that at a time when that regime was loosening its iron grip on society – from 1933 to 1936 – new ideas could find adoption, policy options could be pressed from below with some chance of success. But the rapid and decisive closure of the gates in the summer of 1936 as a result of Stalin's concern for his own supremacy, a concern exacerbated by debates over Comintern policy towards Spain, blighted every aspect of Soviet policy and cast a sinister shadow across the more enlightened opposition to fascism in Europe. The resultant terror was not of itself responsible for the collapse of either collective security or Popular Front, though its reverberations undoubtedly made those policies more difficult to pursue. Their collapse was due to the intractability of larger forces. The approaching war was made possible by pressures and fissures in the social and diplomatic fabric of Europe which were already too well advanced after the Depression to be eased and sealed by the time the USSR had accepted the correct diagnosis and embarked in pursuit of the appropriate cure. At moments in the historical process even the most ingenious solutions are utterly ineffective.

Notes

For the early history of the Comintern and Soviet policy the best source is still E. H. Carr, *History of Soviet Russia*, 14 volumes (London, 1950–78).

For the period immediately prior to that under review, see J. Haslam, 'The Comintern and the Origins of the Popular Front 1934–35'. *The Historical Journal*, vol. 22 (1979) no. 3, pp. 673–91, and E. H. Carr, *The Twilight of Comintern 1930–1935* (London, 1982).

Most of the material used for this chapter also appears in J. Haslam, *The Soviet Union and the Struggle for Collective Security in Europe 1933–39* (London, 1984) and in J. Haslam, 'Political Opposition to Stalin and the Origins of the Terror in Russia 1932–36', in *The Historical Journal*, vol. 29 (1986) no. 2, pp. 395–418. An additional source has been P. Spriano, *I comunisti europei e Stalin* (Turin, 1983). The most informative Soviet history of the Comintern in this period is K. K. Shirinya, *Strategiya i taktika Kominterna v bor'be protiv fashizma i voiny (1934–1939 gg.)* (Moscow, 1979). Despite its brevity, E. H. Carr, *The Comintern and the Spanish Civil War* (London, 1984) draws on new sources (Togliatti's secret reports in particular).

Index

161